The Unconditional Freeness of the Gospel

The Unconditional Freeness of the Gospel

In Three Essays. Annotated Edition

by

THOMAS ERSKINE, ESQ. ADVOCATE

Edited and with introductory essay and notes by
Richard L. Leimbach

Source text taken from the unabridged version
printed in 1828 by Waugh and Innes, Edinburgh

WIPF & STOCK · Eugene, Oregon

THE UNCONDITIONAL FREENESS OF THE GOSPEL
In Three Essays. Annotated Edition

Wipf & Stock
An Imprint of Wipf and Stock Publishers
199 W. 8th Ave., Suite 3
Eugene, OR 97401

www.wipfandstock.com

PAPERBACK ISBN: 978-1-6667-5638-8
HARDCOVER ISBN: 978-1-6667-5639-5
EBOOK ISBN: 978-1-6667-5640-1

Cataloguing-in-Publication data:

Names: Erskine, Thomas, 1788–1870 [author]. | Leimbach, Richard L. [editor]

Title: The unconditional freeness of the gospel : in three essays. annotated edition / Thomas Erskine, edited and with an introductory essay and notes by Richard L. Leimbach.

Description: Eugene, OR: Wipf & Stock Publishers, 2023 | Includes bibliographical references.

Identifiers: ISBN 978-1-6667-5638-8 (paperback) | ISBN 978-1-6667-5639-5 (hardcover) | ISBN 978-1-6667-5640-1 (ebook)

Subjects: LCSH: Erskine, Thomas, 1788–1870 | Grace (Theology) | Forgiveness—Biblical teaching | Forgiveness—Religious aspects—Christianity | Atonement—History of doctrines

Classification: BT790 E75 2023 (paperback) | BT790 (ebook)

03/20/23

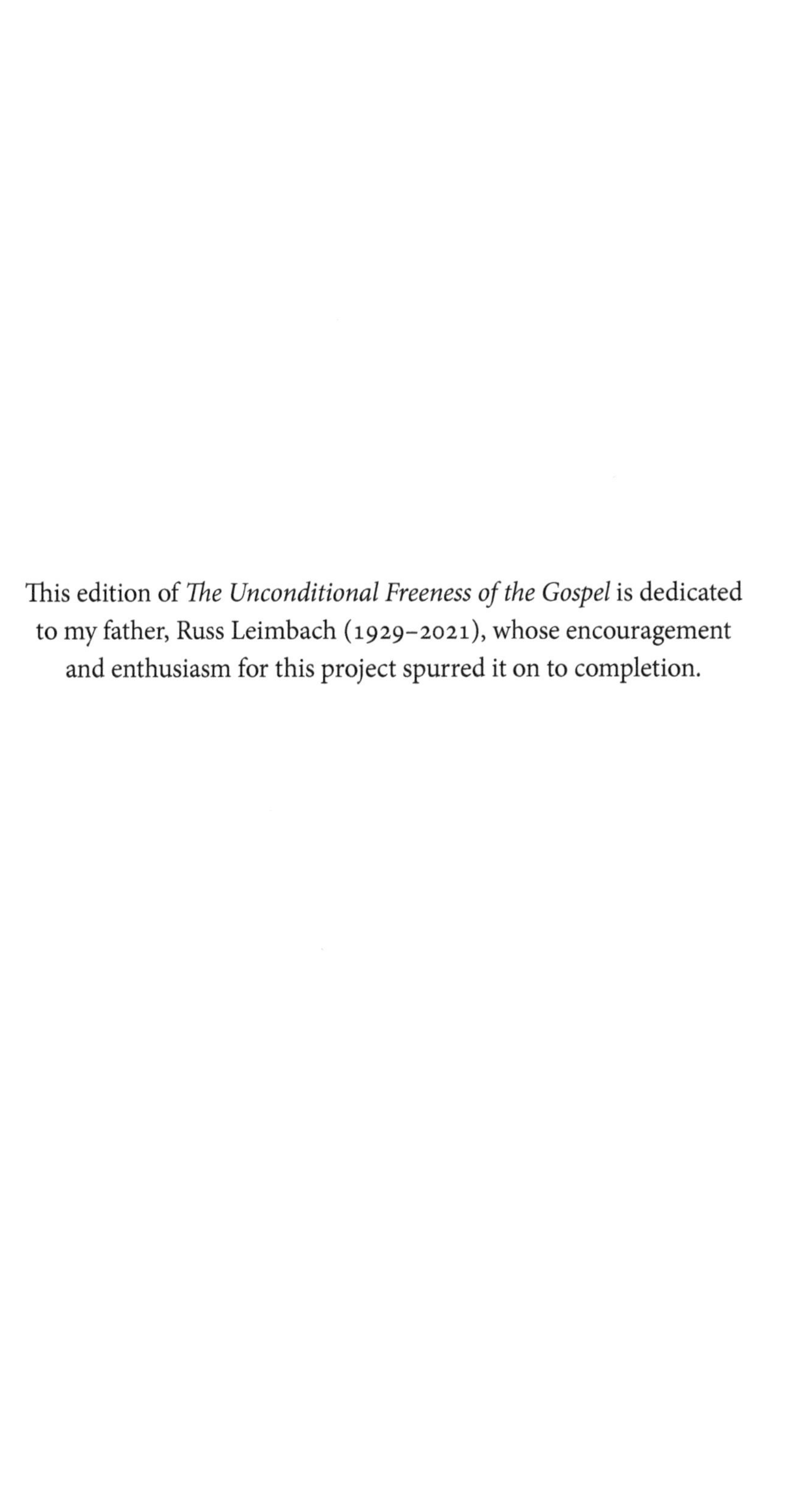

This edition of *The Unconditional Freeness of the Gospel* is dedicated to my father, Russ Leimbach (1929–2021), whose encouragement and enthusiasm for this project spurred it on to completion.

Contents

Permissions

All Scripture quotations unless otherwise noted are taken from the King James Version.

Scripture quotations marked DBH have been taken from *The New Testament: A Translation*®. (DBH), Copyright © 2017 by David Bentley Hart.

Scripture quotations marked ESV are from the ESV® Bible (*The Holy Bible, English Standard Version*®), copyright © 2001 by Crossway, a publishing ministry of Good News Publishers. Used by permission. All rights reserved. The ESV text may not be quoted in any publication made available to the public by a Creative Commons license. The ESV may not be translated into any other language.

Scripture quotations marked HCSB are taken from the Holman Christian Standard Bible®, Used by Permission HCSB ©1999,2000,2002,2003,2009 Holman Bible Publishers. Holman Christian Standard Bible®, Holman CSB®, and HCSB® are federally registered trademarks of Holman Bible Publishers.

Scripture quotations marked MSG are taken from *The Message*, copyright © 1993, 2002, 2018 by Eugene H. Peterson. Used by permission of NavPress. All rights reserved. Represented by Tyndale House Publishers.

Scriptures taken from *Holy Bible, New International Version*®, NIV®. Copyright © 1973, 1978, 1984 by Biblica, Inc™. Used by permission of Zondervan. All rights reserved worldwide. www.zondervan.com.

Scripture taken from the *New King James Version*®. (NKJV), Copyright © 1982 by Thomas Nelson. Used by permission. All rights reserved.

Scripture quotations taken from the (NASB®) *New American Standard Bible*®, Copyright © 1960, 1971, 1977, 1995, 2020 by The Lockman Foundation. Used by permission. All rights reserved. www.lockman.org.

Scriptures taken from the *New Revised Standard Version Bible* (NRSV), copyright 1989, Division of Christian Education of the National Council of the Churches of Christ in the United States of America. Used by permission. All rights.

Scripture taken from *The New Testament for Everyone*®. (NTE), Copyright © Nicholas Thomas Wright 2011, 2018, 2019. Published by Society for Promoting Christian Knowledge (SPCK).

Editor's Preface

I first want to explain how this edition of Thomas Erskine's book *The Unconditional Freeness of the Gospel* came about before going into how it was produced, why it needed to be edited, and why I felt it could benefit from being annotated.

Recently I came across an article I had clipped from a Christian magazine thirteen years ago.[1] I am not usually one to cut articles from magazines, so I was curious to see why I had saved this one. It was an article about forgiveness and faith. In it, the author, theologian C. Baxter Kruger, had declared that Thomas Erskine's book remains one of the most important books he had ever read. The reason he gave was that it solved a critical and practical theological problem for him.

He said that, according to Erskine, the gospel is the good news that God has forgiven the human race. Forgiveness is to be proclaimed as an accomplished fact. It is universal. It is finished. It includes the whole race of humanity. And it is unconditional. Then he added, "Many, of course, believe this to be the plain truth of the gospel. I know I do. Yet there are many others who are deeply troubled by such an unconditional message."

As I read through the article afresh, I remembered why I had saved it. I had wrestled with questions of my own along these same lines. Questions like: Is God's forgiveness a freely given act of grace or is it contingent on us in some way? Nothing made the Pharisees angrier than when Jesus told people their sins were forgiven. He forgave people who didn't even ask to be. I had to wonder, was Jesus able to do something that God the Father couldn't or wouldn't? When Jesus prayed

---

1. "Forgiveness and Faith" by Dr. C. Baxter Kruger originally appeared in the February/March 2008 issue of *Christian Odyssey*. A PDF copy of the article may be obtained from https://archive.gci.org/files/CO1202.pdf.

from the cross, "Father, forgive them for they know not what they do," was he praying only for those who played a part in his crucifixion or was he praying for the whole human race?

It is probably clear from my questions that my own thoughts were already going in the same direction as Erskine's, but I could understand why many would find Erskine's claim troubling. If God can freely forgive sinners and has already forgiven the whole human race, then why does the Bible have so much to say about our need to repent and believe the gospel? And why would it matter how we live our lives now? Also, what about heaven? If God's forgiveness is universal, wouldn't that mean everyone gets a free pass? So, I, just as much as all those who might be troubled by Erskine's claim, wanted to know how Erskine would answer these objections.

Dr. Kruger concluded his article by saying that the good news of God's unconditional forgiveness is like spiritual medicine for our devastated souls. "For it shouts to us that we are loved forever, accepted and embraced by the Father himself. . . . Believing in our Father's love and forgiveness is to take the spiritual medicine that heals our pain-riddled souls. Refusing to believe in our Father's love never changes the fact that we are loved and forgiven; but it leaves our souls unhealed."

Wow! I thought. If Erskine is right, this is truly good news and something that needs to be shared with the whole world. Isn't it because of feelings of guilt and shame that so many are afraid to run to God's open arms? Wouldn't knowing that He is not angry with us and has already forgiven us change everything?

I immediately set out to find a copy of Erskine's book and read it for myself. I can usually find any book I want on the internet, but what I hoped to find was a Kindle version of the book. Shelf space for books is in short supply in my house, so I buy Kindle eBooks whenever possible. Failing that, I felt sure I could get a copy of the book through Google Books. The Library Project has done a remarkable job of creating PDF copies of books in the public domain and making them available for free to readers. The drawback is, like most people, I prefer not to have to read a book on a computer. Another drawback is that PDFs are like photocopies. They can be no better than the original, and the print in old books is sometimes smudgy, faint, or printed in a hard to read typeface.

When I checked Amazon, I found I had the normal three choices. I could buy the book as a hardback, paperback, or for the Kindle. I was happy until I read the fine print so to speak.

Of the three, the hardback reproduction was the only complete copy of Erskine's book. Both the paperback and the Kindle ebook were highly abridged versions of the original. I settled for reading a PDF copy of the original on my computer. At least it was the full text, and I could get my hands on a copy immediately.

When I read Erskine's book, I came to the same conclusion as did Dr. Kruger. *The Unconditional Freeness of the Gospel* was one of the most important books I had ever read. I was also convinced that this book in its entirety should be made available in a form that is easy to read so many more people could read it. That is how the idea of publishing an unabridged version of the book to Kindle came about.

My first challenge was to produce a Word document from the original book. OCR (optical character reader) software was a great invention, but if anyone thinks it will take the work out of converting a printed book into a Word document, they should think again. What the software produced was a long narrow column of words, almost like a ticker tape, and left me the with work of removing hundreds of unwanted carriage returns, spaces, and blank lines. The tiny dots of ink splatter that were the normal byproduct of printing in the 1800s were interpreted as periods, hyphens, apostrophes, and other strange characters. (If I have missed any, please forgive me.) Then there were the many lines that had been converted to complete gibberish. They, of course, all had to be retyped and checked against the original text word by word.

As you might surmise, if I did not think *The Unconditional Freeness of the Gospel* was worth the effort, I would not have gone to all this trouble, but with every line-by-line, word-by-word reading of the book, I was becoming more convinced that Erskine's book was one of the greatest expositions of God's love and the transforming power of gospel that I had ever read. I wanted everyone to read and appreciate it as I did.

But that was going to be a problem. Some who had read the original said that they had had trouble with the book's archaic language and style. This is a valid complaint. Erskine frequently used words and phrases that would be unfamiliar to most modern readers. At times, even his word order seemed strange, and it was not uncommon for him to slip into King James English when alluding to some passage of scripture.

I decided something had to be done about this. So, I set out to modernize the book's language without changing its meaning. My first step was to replace all the archaic words and phrases with their modern equivalents. For the purists, whenever a word was replaced, I noted the original word in a footnote. In a few cases, I left the unfamiliar word in place and inserted its definition in brackets.

If Erskine is typical of other authors of his day, then people back then must have had something against short sentences. Most of the time, Erskine's sentences flow quite naturally, and even though they may be unusually long, this does not seem a very great distraction, so I left them untouched. However, in cases where he had strung short sentences together with semicolons, I separated them.

As to spelling, I pursued the course of changing English spellings to American and antiquated to modern. Phrases like "nothing else than" were changed to "nothing other than"; "viz." was replaced with "that is to say" or "in other words." Style wise, I kept Erskine's way of using dashes to tie thoughts together. In matters of punctuation, I removed dozens of commas and added others where modern grammar dictated. As was the custom of his day, Erskine used Roman numerals in all his biblical references. These I have converted to Arabic numerals for the sake of the modern reader. To make for consistency of style with the main text of the book, I have used caps for divine pronouns in quotations taken from the King James Version of the Bible.

Erskine quotes extensively from the King James Bible. There were, of course, few other options in his day. That means there may be some archaic words and expressions in the quotations, but I thought it best not to try to substitute a more modern translation. If you are not used to reading 1611 King James English, stay with it. It gets easier with familiarity.

All the footnotes and annotations found in this edition of *The Unconditional Freeness of the Gospel* are my own. My primary reason for deciding to add footnotes was to tell the reader where to find the scriptures quoted in the book, something the author seldom does.

Next, I saw the need to add explanatory notes. This was especially true in the second essay where Erskine uses the word "forfeiture" about twenty times in a way that would make little sense to most readers without some sort of explanation.

Other notes were added as deemed helpful. I added a note to the first page when I considered how odd his opening paragraphs would seem without the understanding that Erskine was addressing a heated debate in his own day—a debate between the holiness movement and those who believed in justification by faith without works. Is faith all that is required of us or does God want us to become Christlike? If you want to skip to the next subtitle, I say go right ahead, but please do not let the way the book begins stop you from reading it.

Finally, it is time to say something about the structure of Erskine's book. The original book was divided into three solid blocks of text labeled Essay I, II, and III. There were no chapter titles or subtitles. I have added both in an effort to help the reader navigate the text and to follow Erskine's chain of thought more easily.

My prayer is that the words of this book will cause many more people to run headlong into the open arms of God our Father and experience the love and forgiveness that has been waiting there for every one of us all along.

Richard Leimbach
July 22, 2022

Thomas Erskine of Linlathen.

Introduction to Thomas Erskine (1788–1870)

RICHARD L. LEIMBACH

Thomas Erskine of Linlathen has been described as "possibly the most theologically astute layperson to write theology in the 19th century."[1] Although largely forgotten today, historians have deemed him to have been the central figure in the Scottish theological awakening that

1. Young, "Thomas Erskine," lines 107–8.

occurred between 1820 and 1830,[2] and along with Englishman Samuel Taylor Coleridge to have been one of the two most "instrumental in the regeneration of British theology in the nineteenth century."[3]

His first biographer, Henry Henderson, said that as a thinker as well as a personal force, he was an "extraordinary phenomenon," especially coming as he did from "the stiff Calvinistic soil of Scotland."[4] In Henderson's view (and in the view of successive biographers), Erskine's influence as a teacher of spiritual Christianity, meaning a Christianity that is lived, has been "great, greater than he has ever received credit for."[5]

To Henderson's mind, if anyone were to judge Erskine's influence by the extent to which his thoughts had entered the mind of the age and had become enlisted among the ruling ideas of the world, Erskine's influence would be unmistakable. He said,

> If we single out any one of his favorite topics in the department of Ethics or Theology, the peculiar treatment of which appeared so revolutionary at the period of its first publication, it may be confidently asserted that there are few teachers of the present day exercising religious influence over their fellowmen who are not indebted to him. His influence has been great and helpful even on those matters on which, in the opinion of many, the conclusions which Erskine reached were rash and unwarranted.[6]

Henderson did not explain what those conclusions were that so many considered "rash and unwarranted." We, on the other hand, will take a moment to investigate because they will serve to introduce Erskine's story and at the same time elicit comments on one of Erskine's key themes. Afterwards, we will return to those ideas that had, as Henderson put it, entered "the mind of the age."

When Thomas Erskine wrote *The Unconditional Freeness of the Gospel*, he was already a well-known and celebrated author. His first book, *Remarks on the Internal Evidence for the Truth of Revealed Religion*, written in 1820, had been well received in his Scottish homeland as an exceptionally fine work of Christian apologetics.[7] In the language of our

2. Drummond and Bulloch, *The Scottish Church* 194, 199; Storr, *Development of English Theology* 353; Story *Apostolic Ministry*, 306–8.

3. Franks, *History*, Vol. II, 379

4. Henderson, *Erskine*, ix.

5. Henderson, *Erskine*, 132.

6. Henderson, *Erskine*, 125–26.

7. Needham, *Thomas Erskine*, 55.

day, it was a runaway best seller. Sales of the book were unprecedented. In the first ten years, it went through nine editions and was eagerly read in both England and America as well as on the European continent when it was later published in French (1822) and German (1825).[8]

His second book, *An Essay on Faith* (1822), was also well received and only served to further enhance Erskine's reputation as an innovative thinker and theologian. While it never reached quite as wide a circulation as his first, it too went through multiple editions and was translated into French.[9]

But when *Unconditional Freeness* was published in 1828, there was a marked change in the public's reception of Erskine's books. Some, like Thomas Chalmers,[10] a leader of the Church of Scotland and a friend of Erskine's, found it to be a "most delightful book,"[11] but others, like Andrew Thomson,[12] founder and editor of the influential *Edinburgh Christian Instructor*, panned it.

While Thomson did appreciate Erskine's "deep piety and devoted attention to the cause of pure and undefiled Christianity," he objected to the way that Erskine gave new meanings to old terms, important and elementary terms, such as salvation, justification, heaven and hell, and eternal life. These new meanings were in his opinion "fanciful, unwarrantable, and dangerous innovations."[13] What Thomson considered dangerous innovations, however, would be seen by others as helpful and welcomed attempts to pioneer new ways forward in a system of theology that had become stale, stagnant, and largely irrelevant to the personal lives of many everyday people.

Erskine did not discount the theological work of those who had gone before, but he contended that that work was not finished with the Westminster Confession.[14] In a letter to Thomas Chalmers, Erskine

---

8. Reid, *Influence*, 11, 193, 282; Hanna, *Letters*, 576–77.

9. Winslow, *Thomas Erskine*, 9.

10. Thomas Chalmers (1780–1847) was a Scottish minister, professor of theology, and a leader of both the Church of Scotland and of the Free Church of Scotland. He has been called "Scotland's greatest nineteenth-century churchman."

11. Needham, *Thomas Erskine*, 195.

12. Andrew Mitchell Thomson (1779–1831) was the pastor of St. George's Church, Edinburgh, and leader of the evangelical party in the Church of Scotland.

13. Winslow, *Thomas Erskine*, 18–19.

14. The Westminster Confession, also known as the Confession of Faith, was a document drawn up in 1647 and held to be the standard of orthodoxy by almost all Scottish churches in Erskine's day.

wrote, "Surely the Westminster divines did not exhaust the Bible; and if they had the Spirit, surely the divines of our day are not excluded from the Spirit, and if so, they ought to thank God for what light was seen before and press on the further light in the strength of the Spirit."[15]

One of those "dangerous innovations" was Erskine's thoughts on the meaning of salvation. Erskine argued that if we believe our Savior's mission to earth was to save people from their sins, then we must also believe that salvation means not salvation from punishment but *from sin itself.*[16] Salvation is what takes place as we grow in sympathy with God and begin to love righteousness and hate evil as He does. It is what happens when we die to self and live to God. It is the truth of God abiding richly and effectively in the soul. And above all, salvation means a growing personal acquaintance with God in the here and now as attested by Jesus when He prayed shortly before His crucifixion, "[T]his is eternal life, that they may know thee, the only true God, and Jesus Christ whom thou hast sent" (John 17:3).[17]

All of this was quite different and more than a bit troubling for those used to viewing salvation from the other end of the telescope. For most, salvation was not about the present or about sanctification. It was about the future. Salvation was the reward that the faithful would receive *after* they died and "went to heaven." The faithful were, as understood in Calvinistic Scotland, an exclusive group. They were the elect—those of mankind chosen by God from before the foundation of the world and predestined to eternal life.[18] Only the elect were the recipients of God's saving grace.[19] Everyone else was destined (or predestined) to damnation.

From the mid-1600s on, the Westminster Shorter Catechism, had been the staple of instruction for all Scottish children, which meant its teachings were almost indelibly etched into the minds of anyone growing up in Scotland. To the question, "What does every sin deserve?," it replied, "Every sin deserveth God's wrath and curse, both in this life, and that which is to come." Questions and Answers 19–21 outlined the idea that because of the fall, every human being was destined for the eternal

---

15. Winslow, *Thomas Erskine*, 46–47.

16. Erskine, *Spiritual Order*, 243.

17. Winslow, *Thomas Erskine*, 1–2.

18. *Westminster Confession*, Ch. 3, para. 5.

19. "Neither are any other redeemed by Christ, effectually called, justified, adopted, sanctified, and saved, but the elect only" (*Westminster Confession of Faith*, Ch. 3, para. 6).

torments of hell, that is, unless they had a Redeemer, but Jesus Christ was not everyone's Redeemer. He was only the Redeemer of the elect.

> All mankind by their fall lost communion with God, are under his wrath and curse, and so made liable to all miseries in this life, to death itself, and to the pains of hell forever. God having, out of his mere good pleasure, from all eternity, elected some to everlasting life, did enter into a covenant of grace, to deliver them out of the estate of sin and misery, and to bring them into an estate of salvation by a Redeemer. The only Redeemer of God's elect is the Lord Jesus Christ.

The official teaching of the Church of Scotland was that Jesus was not the Savior of all people because not everyone had been called to salvation.[20] From the pulpit and in writing, the ministers of the Church roundly denied that there was in God a love for all men.[21] God loved some and withheld his love from others based not on anything they had done or ever would do but entirely on the good pleasure of His will, a will represented by the Confession of Faith as simply an arbitrary will.

To Thomas Erskine, this was a very dark view of God's character and of His disposition towards humanity, and it was not at all like the God Erskine found revealed in Jesus or in all the Bible for that matter. He wrote,

> Throughout even the Old Testament, God is more constantly presented to us as a Father than in any other character, and in the New, our Lord speaks of it as the chief purpose of His appearance in the world, to reveal His Father as the Father of the whole human race. In both, frequent appeals are made to our sense of the love and desires and obligations of an earthly parent towards his children in order to impress on us the nature of the relation in which God stands to each one of us, and very frequently, these appeals are accompanied with the assurance that the love of the human parent is but a faint reflection of the love of the Heavenly Father. What can be more touching than the appeal in the prophet Isaiah? "Can a woman forget her sucking child, that she should not have compassion on the son of her womb? yea, they may forget, yet will not I forget thee."[22] The parallel passage in the New Testament is this: "If ye then, being

---

20. *Westminster Confession*, Ch. 10, para. 1.

21. Needham, *Thomas Erskine*, 5–6.

22. Isa 49:15.

> evil, know how to give good gifts to your children, how much more will your Heavenly Father give!"[23]

The question Erskine leaves hanging is this: if God is more loving than any earthly father, what grounds do we have to believe He would withhold any of His gifts (grace, mercy, peace, love, and forgiveness) from any of His children? The answer is none.

In the Scriptures, God has declared his love for all people without exception. Erskine wrote in *Unconditional Freeness*, "God so loved the world (the whole world—all the race of Adam) as to give His only begotten Son for them."[24] That meant that the Father's love was universal, and that God was not just a father to some but the Father of *all*.

Throughout the seventeenth century and continuing into the eighteenth, the sovereignty of God dominated religious thought in Scotland. "The Lord reigneth" was the central idea that pervaded the whole of the Scottish theological system. God was the supreme King. He was our King and Lawgiver, and we are His subjects. Our relationship to God was understood as being primarily governmental, and as church historian R. H. Story speaking before the Assembly of the Church of Scotland in 1903 put it, "The Fatherhood of God was ignored. The Fatherly love was never spoken of; it might not exist for all that was found in the theological system of the Confession of Faith."[25]

It was in this setting and for the purpose of restoring the theological balance between the sovereignty of God on the one hand and the Fatherhood of God on the other that Erskine wrote *The Unconditional Freeness of the Gospel.* God is indeed sovereign, but it is not enough to say that He is Lord of all, Creator and Ruler of the whole world without adding that His rule is unlike that of any earthly king. His sovereignty, unlike theirs, is based on love—the love of a father for his children. The God that Jesus came to reveal is *first and foremost* a Father, and not just a Father to some but a Father to all.

Erskine wrote, "Jesus came preaching peace by declaring his Father to be the common Father of men, prodigals and all."[26] "He came to seek and save the lost, by declaring to them the Father's heart, and as soon as they know that heart, they are glad. They rejoice in salvation, but whilst

---

23. Hanna, *Letters*, 425.

24. Erskine, *Unconditional Freeness*, 39.

25. Reid, *Influence*, 190.

26. Erskine, *Doctrine of Election*, 569.

they continue ignorant of God's heart, they continue to be without eternal life in them. . . . God's heart is a heart of forgiving love to us before we believe, but we cannot enjoy God, which is full salvation, without knowing or believing what His heart is to us."[27]

For Erskine, there was nothing that revealed the Father's heart towards all humankind more than the fact that He gave His Son to be the "propitiation for our sins, and not for ours only, but also for the sins of the whole world."[28] Christ did not die so that God might be induced to love us. He died *because* God *already* loved us. His sacrifice on the cross was the *outcome*, and not the *cause* of God's love for humanity, and the very fact that Christ died for and on behalf of all sinners means that all sinners are pardoned—all are forgiven. "The pardon of the gospel then is in effect a declaration on the part of God to every individual sinner in the whole world that His holy compassion embraces him, and that the blood of Jesus Christ has atoned for his sins."[29]

Lest there be any misunderstanding, Erskine wanted to make it clear that pardon was not to be confused with salvation. Pardon only opens the door to God and invites sinners in. Unless a sinner knows that he or she is forgiven and returns to God and begins walking with Him, God's love and forgiveness are to them useless.

> The love of God abiding in the heart and governing the will of the creature is its salvation—there is no other salvation than this, and therefore while the pardon that is the proclamation of God's love remains on the outside of the heart, while it does not enter in, it produces no salvation. . . . The pardon remains always the same—the access always remains open. The invitation is always urgent, but those who do not come in are not transformed.[30]

The gospel to Erskine was the good news that all are included in God's universal love. God's grace, love, and forgiveness are free to all, and the unconditional freeness of the gospel ought to be preached to every soul under the sun. The truth of the gospel is that God is *for* us. He has always been for us, and there has never been a time when He was not for us *even in our worst state.* God does not love us or pardon us on account of anything we have done or believed. "[F]or it was while we were yet

27. Letter to Monsieur Gaussen, 7 December 1832, *Letters*, 191.

28. 1 John 2:2.

29. Erskine, *Unconditional Freeness*, 38.

30. Erskine, *Unconditional Freeness*, 39.

enemies and unbelievers that Christ died for us, but the belief of his love and of the gift that his love has bestowed will give a confidence that we are dearly welcome to him—that we are his accepted ones—his adopted children."[31] He says to every individual, "You are my child. I love you, and I don't want to lose you."

As one biographer put it, the message of the gospel, according to Erskine, was not "if you repent and believe God will love and forgive you," but precisely "God already loves you and has forgiven you, therefore repent and believe."[32]

Already we have heard Erskine express his views on several of his favorite topics—the universal Fatherhood of God, the universal atonement of Christ, the freeness of the gospel, and the assurance that no matter who we are, we are loved by God—all views that when he first presented them were vociferously denounced as dangerous, unwarranted, and heretical, and yet these are the same views that Henderson, writing at the turn of the twentieth century, could say had become enlisted among the ruling ideas of the Christian world.

All these themes are commonplace in Christian thought today. Erskine's great theme of the Fatherhood of God has become practically the viewpoint of modern theology.[33] Yet as Erskine scholar Don Horrocks notes, "Erskine's pioneering initiative in seeking constructively to redress the theological balance [between God's sovereignty and God's Fatherhood] was initially without contemporary precedent in Scotland."[34]

There had already been hints of unrest among the rank and file of the Church of Scotland as underscored by the Marrow controversy of the early 1700s. The "Marrowmen"[35] had contended that Christ had died for all and that God, moved by His universal love, had made the gift of Christ the Savior available to all.[36] But in 1720, the General Assembly of the Church determined that these ideas were inconsistent with the Confession of Faith and roundly condemned them, despite the fact that it could be and

---

31. Erskine, *Unconditional Freeness*, 72.

32. Hart, *Teaching Father*, 27.

33. Horrocks, *Laws of the Spiritual Order*, 43–44.

34. Horrocks, *Laws of the Spiritual Order*, 27–28.

35. The Marrowmen were Scottish divines who had read and agreed with Englishman Edward Fisher's 1645 book titled *The Marrow of Modern Divinity*.

36. Needham, *Thomas Erskine*, 472.

was argued that the propositions the Assembly had condemned were both scriptural and plainly taught by many orthodox Scottish divines.[37]

A hundred years later brings us to Erskine's time when once again there was an undercurrent of unrest, though of a different sort. Historian R. H. Story described it as having to do with a "deepening spiritual consciousness," which the religion of the land was unable to satisfy, a spiritual consciousness that "could not accept as a veracious theory of Atonement one which excluded from its scope the vast majority of human beings." He said that people were looking for a "more direct and personal application of the Gospel than the ordinary preaching commonly offered, and . . . an exposition of the Atonement which should evolve a deeper moral and spiritual meaning than that of the ordinary doctrine." Story concluded by saying, "The earliest, and in some respects the most deeply spiritual and original, representative of this unrest and wider outlook was a layman, Thomas Erskine of Linlathen," who along with his friend and fellow-laborer John McLeod Campbell were "the pioneers of the movement, which has ultimately broken the gloomy dominion of the theology that had been so cramped in its growth by the shackles of Westminster that its continued influence would have, sooner or later, extinguished the spiritual and intellectual liberty without which an apostolic ministry becomes impossible."[38]

At this point, I need to pause and explain the connection between Thomas Erskine and John McLeod Campbell. It is nearly impossible to tell either man's story without mentioning the other. The two will forever be linked in the annals of Scottish church history.

Campbell was the young pastor of the Parish of Row.[39] In later years, he would recount how "working apart and without any interchange of thought," he had arrived at the same conclusions as Thomas Erskine.[40] The difference was, unlike Erskine, Campbell was a member of the clergy and answerable to the Church of Scotland for what he believed and taught.

Campbell's own thoughts on God's unconditional, forgiving love for sinners and the assurance of faith had developed out of a pastoral concern for his parishioners. In Row, he found a people who did not doubt

37. See Wikipedia article the "Marrow Controversy."

38. Story, *Apostolic Ministry*, 307–8.

39. Row, now spelled Rhu, was a village in the county of Dunbartonshire, Scotland, twenty-four miles north-west of Glasgow and sixty-two miles almost due west of Edinburgh.

40. Horrocks, *Laws of the Spiritual Order*, 14.

Christ's power and willingness to save, nor did they doubt the freeness of the gospel, yet they lacked the peace and assurance that comes from knowing and believing that they themselves were the object of God's love.

This lack of assurance of God's love for every individual should not have been totally unexpected. The Westminster Confession taught that God's love and forgiveness were only available to those who already had faith, and the only way of knowing whether one had faith was *retrospectively* by discovering the "evidences" or "fruits of the Spirit" in one's own life—something that the Confession said could be a long and difficult thing to do.[41]

Campbell, as the new pastor of Row, soon saw as his chief task that of helping his parishioners move past this barrier of spiritual introspection that they had erected between themselves and trusting Christ and "to fix their attention on the love of God revealed in Christ, and to get themselves into the mental attitude of looking at God to learn His feelings towards them, not at themselves to consider their feelings towards Him."[42]

It was a great disappointment to Campbell that the gospel message that Christ's death revealed God's saving love for all men was not as readily accepted by his flock as he had hoped. Instead of producing a joyful confidence in Christ, many found it difficult to accept the idea that God's grace and love were free to all and were not conditioned on any goodness on their own part.

Campbell's troubles with the Church of Scotland began in 1827 when some summer visitors to Row returned south to Glasgow and reported what they had heard him preach. As the result of the attention and excitement generated by these reports, a paper was read in support of the traditional doctrine of assurance by "evidences" at Glasgow's theological society. Campbell was present and was invited to respond, which he did hoping that those hearing him speak would meditate on what he was able to say.[43]

What happened next shows that Campbell was still a bit naïve about how difficult it is to change men's minds, especially in matters of doctrinal belief. Soon after the theological society's paper was read, Campbell had the occasion to give a public sermon before one of the charitable institutions of Glasgow with most of Glasgow's ministers in attendance.

41. Horrocks, *Laws of the Spiritual Order*, 99–100.

42. Needham, *Thomas Erskine*, 469.

43. Campbell, *Reminiscences*, 20.

Campbell took it as an opportunity to explicate the practical importance of the assurance of faith.

The result was almost predictable. Campbell had hoped that his explanation would remove prejudices and commend men to the truth, but he said that they, on the other hand, "had calculated on my being changed by what had come from them, and in consequence were much offended to hear me so shortly after state so fully what they had condemned."[44]

The growing opposition to Campbell's teaching on assurance only drove him deeper into the Scriptures. He wrote,

> The controversy in which I was constantly engaged in almost all my intercourse with my brethren urged me to examine narrowly the foundation furnished by the communications made in the Gospel for Assurance of Faith. This led directly to the closer consideration of the extent of the Atonement, and the circumstances in which mankind had been placed by the shedding of the blood of Christ; and it soon appeared to me manifest that unless Christ had died for all and unless the Gospel announced Him as the gift of God to every human being, so that there remained nothing to be done to give the individual a title to rejoice in Christ as his own Saviour, there was no foundation in the record of God for the Assurance which I demanded, and which I saw to be essential to true holiness. The next step therefore was my teaching as the subject matter of the Gospel, Universal Atonement and Pardon through the blood of Christ.[45]

In the winter of 1828, Campbell was invited to deliver a sermon in Edinburgh at which time Thomas Erskine was in attendance. After the sermon, Erskine is reported to have said to the person next to him, "I have heard today from that pulpit what I believe to be the true gospel."[46] This fortuitous meeting between the two was to become the start of a lifelong friendship, and in retrospect, it may well be seen as God's encouraging hand on the lives of two men who were about to face together some of the most trying times of their lives, and that for what they both firmly believed to be the true gospel.

In January of 1830, Campbell wrote to his sister in India that the seasonal visitors to Row had gone away "rejoicing in the Lord" and had returned home "spreading the good news" that they had heard him

44. Campbell, *Reminiscences*, 20–21.

45. Campbell, *Reminiscences*, 24.

46. Hart, *Teaching Father*, 29.

preach. The reaction was by this time something that Campbell had come to expect: the pulpits of Edinburgh and Glasgow were alive with sermons against what was now being called the "Row heresy."[47]

In March, eight parishioners of Row were persuaded to make a formal charge of heresy against their pastor to the Presbytery. This resulted in an official delegation arriving in July to hear Campbell preach. By September, his case had been heard by the Presbytery and the libel (indictment) proven "relevant."[48] At which point, Campbell's only option apart from immediately leaving the ministry was to appeal his case to the Synod of Glasgow and Ayr.

On April 13th of 1831, Campbell's case came before the Synod. The charge against him was that he held and repeatedly promulgated "contrary to the Holy Scriptures and the Confession of Faith approven by the General Assemblies of the Church of Scotland" the "doctrine of universal atonement and pardon through the grace of Christ" and also "the doctrine that assurance is one of the essence of faith and necessary to salvation." The indictment continued,

> [Y]ou have declared that God has forgiven the sins of all mankind whether they believe it or not: That in consequence of the death of Christ, the sins of every individual of the human race are forgiven; That it is sinful and absurd to pray for an interest [advantage, benefit] in Christ, because all mankind have an interest in Christ already: And that no man is a Christian unless he is positively assured of his salvation.[49]

For those closely following the proceedings, the similarity between Campbell's ideas and Erskine's was unmistakable, so much so, that in the minds of many, Thomas Erskine was the true source of the "Row heresy." Campbell was the clergyman on trial, but from the pulpit and in the press, through pamphlets, articles, and books, it was Thomas Erskine who was the target of much of the Scottish religious world's wrath. So, when on Wednesday 25th May 1831, the General Assembly of the Church of Scotland deposed John McLeod Campbell, minister of the gospel at Row, it was as much a judgment against Erskine as it was Campbell.

Both men had been accused of teaching contrary to the Scriptures, but it is worth noting that at his trial, Campbell had requested that he

47. Campbell, *Reminiscences*, 31–32.

48. Winslow, *Thomas Erskine*, 34.

49. Winslow, *Thomas Erskine*, 34.

be judged by the light of Scripture and Scripture alone. In response he was told that the "Standards of the Church"—meaning the Westminster Confession—would be the only basis on which his case would be argued. "Any detailed reference to the Scriptures" was "altogether unnecessary."[50]

Campbell's carefully worded reaction to this decision is worth repeating:

> If you show me that anything I have taught is inconsistent with the Word of God, I shall give it up, and allow you to regard it as a heresy. . . . If a Confession of Faith were something to stint or stop the Church's growth in light and knowledge and to say, "Thus far shalt thou go and no further," then a Confession of Faith would be the greatest curse that ever befell a church. Therefore, I distinctly hold that no minister treats the Confession of Faith right if he does not come with it, as a party, to the Word of God, and to acknowledge no other tribunal in matters of heresy than the Word of God. In matters of doctrine no lower authority can be recognized than that of God.[51]

The Church of Scotland could silence its own clergy by depriving them of a license to preach, but Thomas Erskine was not a member of the clergy, and neither was he dependent on anyone for his livelihood. He had inherited the family estate of Linlathen in 1816, making him financially independent. So as one writer for the *Spectator* noted, it "rendered it a matter of no consequence to his outward comfort whether society accepted or condemned his utterances, and so far as the moral courage is concerned of deliberately encountering the prejudices of a whole nation, Erskine showed that he possessed it."[52]

Three more books from Erskine followed *The Unconditional Freeness of the Gospel*. *The Brazen Serpent: Or, Life Coming through Death* was published in 1831, the same year as Campbell's deposition. It was followed by *The Doctrine of Election* in 1837.

Erskine's last book, *The Spiritual Order and Other Papers*, was unfinished when he died, but he had left instructions for this contingency. All the papers that he had ready were to be set in order and sent to the publisher as is. This final book was published in 1871.

Erskine also left specific instructions that an excerpt from *The Spiritual Order* be published separately as a pamphlet immediately on his

50. Hart, *Teaching Father*, 34.

51. Reardon, *Religious Thought*, 299–300.

52. Horrocks, *Laws of the Spiritual Order*, 4.

death. This was done as he requested, and the pamphlet titled "The Purpose of God in the Creation of Man" was printed and distributed in 1870.

I believe the significance of this final piece has too often been overlooked. First, as Erskine's final request, it tells us what he considered to be most important, and secondly, it means that Erskine had come full circle and was ending where his theological journey had begun.

Erskine was around seventeen years old when he read the essays of English Baptist minister, John Foster (1770–1843). It was from Foster that Erskine first heard that God is a loving Father and that the purpose of His love is to educate us as His children—to train us in His own righteous character and thus to make us sharers in His own blessedness.[53] Erskine's reaction to this new understanding was that if life was given for the education of character, then it was a serious matter indeed. It meant that life was the seed-time for eternity and that the purpose of God towards men is not probation, as Erskine once believed, but an educative process that manifests the unchangeable character of God, rather than a particular act.[54] Foster also taught Erskine the need for a deep personal dependence on this loving Father because it was only by continually looking to God for help that we can ever succeed in becoming what He wants us to be.[55]

From this beginning with Foster, it is not hard to see how it soon came to Erskine that there are two views of human life—two views that he said are in principle opposed to each other and lead to opposing conceptions of the character of God and of the relation in which we stand to Him.[56] The one view supposes that God made men so that He afterwards may judge them. The other holds that He judges them so that He may teach them, and that His judgments are instructions.[57]

The first view, Erskine said, holds that we are here in a state of probation—under trial as it were. But that is simply wrong. We are not in a state of trial. We are in a process of education directed by that eternal purpose of love that brought us into being. He went on,

> It is impossible to have a true confidence in God whilst we feel
> ourselves in a state of trial: we must necessarily regard him not
> as a Father but as a Judge, and we must be occupied with the

---

53. Keyser, "A Critical Analysis," 14.

54. Erskine, *Letters*, 278–79; Reid, *Influence*, 245.

55. Keyser, "A Critical Analysis," 14.

56. Erskine, "Purpose of God," 6.

57. Erskine, *Letters*, 393.

thought how we are to pass our trial. We know our own unworthiness, and though we know that we have a Savior, there must still be a degree of alarm in the thought of that judgment seat. But when we have once realized the idea that we are in a process of education, which God will carry on to its fulfilment however long it may take, we feel that the loving purpose of our Father is ever resting on us, and that the events of life are not appointed as testing us whether we will choose God's will or our own, but real lessons to train us into making the right choice. If probation is our thought, then forgiveness or receiving a favorable sentence is our object; if education is our thought, then progress in holiness is our object. If I believe myself in a state of education, every event, even death itself, becomes a manifestation of God's eternal purpose. On the probation system, Christ appears as the deliverer from a condemnation; on the education system, He appears as the deliverer from sin itself."[58]

If there was one thing that Thomas Erskine would want to leave with his readers, I believe it would be what you have just read. Life is not a probation but an education. For Erskine, this principle of education is what lies at the very heart of the gospel because it is what expresses God's loving purpose for creating humanity. As Erskine put it, "I believe that God created man that He might instruct him into a conformity with His own character, and so make him a partner of His own life, the eternal life, which is His will or character."[59]

58. Erskine, *Letters*, 128–29.
59. Erskine, *Letters*, 393.

Part One

The Unconditional Freeness
of the Gospel
(1828)

Forgiveness and Faith: Essay I

Holiness Versus Justification by Faith[1]

I believe that there are many persons who oppose the doctrine of justification by faith from the honest conviction that it opposes the interests of practical holiness or Christian morals. Such persons deserve at least the respect of those who value holiness. They acknowledge the excellency and the obligation of the precepts that describe the Christian character—they are persuaded that any view of Christian doctrine that does not agree with the tendency of these precepts must be incorrect, and as they do not perceive that the doctrine of justification by faith without works has this agreement, they conceive themselves warranted to reject it as a misrepresentation of the language of scripture. Now, I do not think that this class of objectors have been often either kindly or fairly answered. Their case certainly at first sight appears a strong one, and they are in any event entitled to have their statement of it candidly received and discussed. Let us endeavor to do so.

1st, In the first place, they say, by making pardon a free gift irrespective of character, you take away a powerful motive to obedience, and you give the strange and pernicious impression that God is indifferent to right and wrong in his intelligent creatures.

1. Erskine begins his book in a way that may seem odd to readers unfamiliar with a debate that had erupted in his day. The debate was between adherents to the holiness movement, a movement found chiefly among Methodists, but also among Quakers, Anabaptists, and Restorationists, and those who believed that the doctrine of justification by faith meant that Christian holiness was not necessary for salvation.

2dly, We object, they continue, to the propriety of the title that you give to your system. You call it a system of *free salvation*, and you say that it attributes all to God, and yet it is in fact as much hindered with conditions and contains as much of human effort as our own. Faith is in your system what obedience is in ours, and they are both acts of the human mind. You blame us for resting our hopes on the obedience that we can discover in our lives while at the same time you avowedly rest your hopes on the faith that you can discover in your hearts. But you defend yourselves by saying that faith is the gift of God. Well, we also say that obedience is the gift of God. In point of gratuitousness, then, the two systems are thus nearly on a par, that is to say, neither of them is gratuitous except in name. And, in point of moral influence, we would ask whether a system that rests salvation on the belief of any facts whatsoever can be compared with one which rests it on faithful exertion and holy obedience.

3dly, You depreciate practical holiness by all possible means for even when you are compelled to admit that "without holiness no man shall see the Lord,"[2] you do what you can to weaken the force of the admission by saying that the value of holiness arises simply from its being an evidence of the reality of faith and not from any intrinsic quality of its own.

4thly, You do not seem at all agreed as to what is the meaning of faith. Sometimes you make it to consist in trust and confidence in Christ, sometimes in an intelligent assent to the propositions of Christian doctrines, and sometimes in a mere prostration of reason before divine authority or a gulping down of unintelligible obscurities. Now, really you ought to make out to our fullest satisfaction what faith is before you call us to rest on it anything so important as our eternal interests. But whichever of these various kinds of faith you prefer, and we give you your choice, it must be allowed to be but a meagre substitute for universal obedience. If you take the first definition and make faith to consist in trust in Christ, we acknowledge that it is a most necessary feature of the Christian character, but it cannot fill the place of all duties. It is one duty, and we do not exclude it from our system. On the contrary, we inculcate it as a part of that universal obedience of which we consider salvation to be the recompense. As for the other descriptions of faith, we really think that a man might as reasonably rest his hopes before God on his mathematical science or on his stupid credulity.

---

2. Heb 12:14.

5thly, Although we acknowledge that there are passages of Scripture which appear to support your view of the question, yet we maintain that there are also many most unequivocally on our side, and that the general tendency of the whole Bible, as well as the common sense and the common feeling of man, is decidedly with us, and we therefore think that we do not speak without good reason when we say that your system is founded on misconstruction or misinterpretation of the language of Scripture.

These are some of the objections that are usually made to the doctrine of justification by faith. And I cannot help thinking that they are borne out to a considerable extent by the way in which that doctrine is very commonly stated.

It is true that faith is often spoken of by those who profess this doctrine as if it were the substitute of universal obedience, and thus the gratuitousness of the gospel is as much infringed on as by the avowed system of justification by works while at the same time, the importance of obedience, which is at least nominally maintained by this latter system, is undervalued by the former.

It is true also that holiness is sometimes depreciated into a mere evidence of the reality of faith, and thus reason is given for the conclusion that it might be dispensed with if other evidence could be procured.

When the Freeness of Salvation Seems to Vanish

It is true, also, that we differ considerably in our descriptions of faith, which makes it appear as if we were clinging much more to a word than to a thing. When we tell a man that salvation is perfectly gratuitous while at the same time, we tell him that unless he believes the gospel he cannot be saved, we appear to him to be saying *free* and *not free* with one breath. And we increase his difficulties extremely when we add, "except a man be born again, he cannot see the kingdom of God."[3] The gratuitousness of the salvation seems altogether to vanish in the presence of these high and weighty conditions. And yet, if faith and holiness are not appended as conditions of salvation, where is their place in the Christian system? If Christian doctrine is not believed, it can be of no use, and if Christian faith does not produce Christian holiness, it can be of no use either. Are

3. John 3:3.

not faith and holiness then conditions of salvation? And if there are any conditions of salvation, where is its gratuitousness?

Again, if we are saved by faith, what need is there of works? And if holiness is necessary, what is the meaning of salvation by faith alone?

These propositions do not hang well together—there is at least a *seeming* contradiction in them which ought not to be.

I am well aware that there are many Christians who do not perceive these difficulties at all, and who, of course, are not disquieted by them. The object of their contemplation is not a theological system but the great Being whose nature and relation to us form the theme of theology—and their delight is not in the logical coherence of their theory but in spiritual communion with him. Such persons are indeed blessed—and instead of presuming to teach them, I desire to learn from them. But there are persons of a very different description. There are many who are kept at a distance from Christianity altogether by these apparent contradictions, and there are even many real Christians who have suffered much perplexity from them. To such believers and unbelievers, I humbly offer the solution which has satisfied myself.

Rethinking Heaven and Hell

I think that much of the theoretical difficulty on this matter has arisen from the habit of considering heaven merely as a reward and hell merely as a punishment—and pardon as the deliverance from hell and the introduction into heaven. Now the Bible tells us that the kingdom of heaven is "righteousness, and peace, and joy, in the Holy Ghost,"[4] and it describes the future happiness as consisting in likeness to Christ, "we shall be like Him, for we shall see Him as He is."[5] We are told that it shall be said on the last day to those on the right hand, "Enter into the joy of your Lord."[6] This shows that their joy is to be of the same nature as their Lord's. His joy on earth was to do the will of his Father—it was His meat as He himself expresses it—and, now in heaven, his satisfaction consists in "seeing of the travail of his soul,"[7] that is, in seeing the advancement and accomplishment of the objects for which He suffered below—the salvation of

4. Rom 14:17, KJV.

5. 1 John 3:2.

6. Matt 25:21, 23.

7. Isa 53:11.

sinners and the universal increase of holiness and happiness through the universe by the knowledge of the divine character manifested in his own work. Those who enter this joy must also enter into the Savior's likeness—for only holy and loving beings could find their joy in this. Heaven, then, is the name for a character conformed to the will of God—and hell is the name for a character opposed to the will of God. The idea, therefore, of having heaven without holiness is like the idea of having health without being well—it is a contradiction in terms.

Christianity may be considered as a divinely revealed system of medical treatment for diseased spirits.[8] Heaven is the name for health in the soul, and hell is the name for disease, and the design of Christianity is to produce heaven, and to destroy hell.

The Meaning of Pardon

But what is the meaning of *pardon* unless there are rewards and punishments? The very idea of pardon supposes the existence of law and condemnation. Yes, to be sure it does. Christianity is a *remedial* system grafted onto a system *of law*. When man was originally created, the alternatives of life and death were set before him as the consequences of obedience and disobedience to the divine command—that is to say, he was placed under a system of law. He disobeyed and incurred the penalty. But this was not all, for he found that the principle of self-gratification, which had overcome the love of God in his heart and had thus produced the act of disobedience, was in itself a most tremendous and incurable disease, the fruitful source of innumerable ills. It was then that the mercy of God proclaimed the gospel—a gracious dispensation that had respect both to the external or judicial penalty that had been incurred and to the spiritual disease from which the offence had proceeded, for the view of the divine character that it gives in the plan adopted for the deliverance from the external penalty becomes the spiritual remedy that when truly received, works the cure of the spiritual disease and produces heaven in the soul.

Pardon, then, is not heaven—any more than a medicine is health. Pardon is proclaimed freely and universally—it is perfectly gratuitous—it

8. Three years earlier, Erskine had written in an essay titled "Salvation," "A restoration to spiritual health or conformity to the divine character is the ultimate object of God in His dealings with the children of men." For the full quote, please see "Christlikeness, God's Ultimate Objective" in the final chapter of this book.

is unconditional and unlimited—but heaven is limited to those who are sanctified by the belief of the pardon.

Those, therefore, who maintain the gratuitousness of pardon do not at all suppose that God is indifferent to right and wrong in his creatures—because they also maintain that pardon is the spiritual medicine for the removal of sin, and that heaven, or spiritual happiness, is necessarily limited to those whose hearts are healed and sanctified and conformed to the will of God by the belief of the pardon. When Adam fell, he was expelled from Eden, the type of the favorable presence of God and became subject to death with all its dark retinue of wants and pains. This was a heavy sentence, to be excluded from that favor that is better than life,[9] from that smile which gladdens creation—to bear about with us a weight of sorrows along the dreary path of our sickly existence—and then to have our connection with all things to which we may have attached ourselves as green spots in the desert, broken off by an unseen power that forces us away into a dark and unknown abyss.

The Cause of Man's Misery

But suppose that man was relieved from these judicial inflictions while in other respects he remained unchanged—would he be happy? Does the misery of man at this hour arise simply from death and pain and absence from Eden? Would a healthy immortality in a beautiful garden make him happy? Would the presence of God make him happy? Alas, life itself, even abstracted from pain or sickness, is often a heavy burden—and the presence of the holy God, far from being sought as a blessing, would be shunned as a curse by unholy man.

The misery of man, then, does not arise entirely from positive infliction and could not be relieved by the mere removal of judicial penalties.

What is the misery of man? His mind is diseased. He was made to regard and enjoy God as his chief object, and his faculties will not work healthfully in the absence of this object. But he has left God, and he wearies himself in seeking good from created things. The sentiment of the love of God is to his mind what the keystone is to the arch. It falls to ruin without it. And thus, we now see that his reason bewilders him, and his conscience harasses him—his imagination deceives and disquiets

9. An allusion to Ps 63:3. "Because your steadfast love is better than life, my lips will praise you" (NRSV).

him—his passions and affections agitate and torture him. He has a misery wrought into the very elements of his being, independent altogether of positive infliction. This misery is rarely felt in all its force here, and sometimes it is scarcely felt at all in consequence of the occupation and distraction that the mind finds in external things—but when these things are removed, the unhappiness is felt. Hence, the horror of solitary confinement without the means of occupation. Thus also, the misery of the spirit is sometimes even alleviated by external inflictions, because they draw its attention from itself.

When I can lay the blame of my misery on anything external to me, I have hope of a deliverance. I can distinguish between myself and my sorrow. But it is a terrific discovery to make that I am myself my own misery. I had hoped that the source of the evil was somewhere else, and I retreated, as I thought, within myself. But I found that the more I retreated in that direction, the more intense and intolerable the heat became. My own mind was the furnace. This is indeed appalling for how am I to escape from myself? Yes, we carry hell within us, and were we to walk through Eden, we should blast its sweetest flowers. But we dare not walk there. We are afraid of the presence of the holy one—and conscience, like the flaming sword of the cherubim, keeps the soul from God.

Well, how is pardon to cure this misery? We can understand how a pardon may remove an *external infliction*, but how is it to remove this *internal disease*?

The great cause of the disorder and misery that distract the human mind is *averseness or indifference to God*. The love of God, the keystone of the arch, is fallen from its place, and all has in consequence gone to wreck. The sense of sin continually increases this averseness of the heart from God because pollution hates and fears holiness, and an accusing conscience dreads avenging justice. The only medicine that can cure this dreadful and wide-spreading disorder must be something which will replace the keystone in the arch—something that will rekindle love towards God, that will do away fear and inspire confidence.

When the Pardon of the Gospel Meets the Penalties of the Law

Now, the manifestation of the character of God contained in the circumstances of the pardon is exactly fitted for this purpose. It is not merely a deliverance from penalties that we see there. Indeed, the penalties are not cancelled—death still remains, and man toils and sweats still on the outside of Eden. The pardon in the gospel meets the penalties of the law, not by cancelling them, but by associating them with gifts and promises that disarm them of their terrors. Death remains, but there is a promise of a new and endless life beyond the grave. Eden is still barred, and man still eats his bread at the price of labor, but the access into the real presence of God is thrown open. All are invited and urged to come in that they may ask and receive every blessing that God can grant. But these gifts and promises, though great, do not constitute the most striking or characteristic feature of the gospel. The love of God is better than these gifts—He has loved us and given *Himself* for us.[10] The medicinal virtue of the gospel—the virtue that heals the disease of the soul—that destroys enmity and enkindles holy love—that does away with the fear of punishment and at the same time plants and strengthens the fear of sinning, the medicinal virtue that effects this lies in the manifestation of that love of God that passes knowledge,[11] that holy love with which God so loved the world as to give His only begotten Son as an atonement for its sins.

Holy love is the great principle developed in the gospel. It is the union of an infinite abhorrence towards sin and an infinite love towards the sinner. This mysterious history is the mighty instrument with which the Spirit of God breaks the power of sin in the heart and establishes holy gratitude and filial dependence. The belief that the Deity took upon Himself the nature and the penal obligations of the sinner that He might consistently with justice restore his forfeited life and remove the barrier that the offended law had placed between him and the throne of grace[12]—the belief of this must give a new view of the malignity of sin and of its fearful contrariety to the holy character and government of God and must further give a most touching and overpowering view of the compassion of God. It must break the hard heart to think of having rebelled against such a God and such a Father.

---

10. Eph 5:2.

11. Possibly an allusion to Phil 4:7, connecting the peace of mind that comes from peace with God through the love of God. "And the peace of God, which passes all understanding, shall keep your hearts and minds through Jesus Christ."

12. Erskine is here closely following Rom 8:3–4.

An Important Distinction

The distinction which I have remarked between the judicial penalty attached to sin and the spiritual disease produced in the mind by sin on the one side and between the removal of the judicial penalty and the healing of the spiritual disease on the other side, appears to me of very great importance in the scheme of Christianity. The perpetual controversy between faith and works has arisen in a great measure from the neglect of this distinction. I beg the reader's particular attention while I endeavor to explain this. Those who oppose the doctrine of justification by faith without works suppose that pardon or heaven, which they conceive to be the same thing as pardon, is given as a premium for believing the gospel or even perhaps as a premium for surrendering their own reason to the authority of the divine revelation. I ask whether this is not the common notion of those who oppose the doctrine of justification by faith? I am persuaded that it is—and I can at the same time affirm that there is not the slightest foundation for such a notion in any scriptural statement of the doctrine. Christianity holds out no premium for faith at all that is not consistent with the common sense and the common experience of mankind. If I find a mother weeping over the account of the death of her firstborn, which I know to be a false report, am I to be considered as a very adventurous prophet or extravagant promiser if, when I lay before her the proof of his being in perfect health, I make the declaration beforehand that if she believes my news, she will be saved from her sorrow, and that her heart will rejoice? Why, this is no more than what every reasonable being must regard as the necessary consequence of such a belief. Yet it is true that she is saved from her anguish by faith in my story. But her joy is not a premium bestowed on her to reward her belief. It flows naturally out of her belief. Her grief for the supposed death of her child, and her belief that he is alive and well cannot exist in her mind together. Such a faith necessarily heals such a sorrow. Her faith does not restore her son to life—he is alive whether she believes it or not—but his life is no joy to her unless she believes it. Without faith in my story, she could not be saved from her distress. Take another example. A son outrages in a most atrocious manner the feelings of his father. The father banishes him from his house after pronouncing a malediction on him. The son hears of his death soon after and feels his spirit burdened with the curse. He cannot shake himself free of it—he is a miserable wretch. A friend of his father comes to him and tells him that he had seen his father a few hours before his death, and that he had heard him express the warmest affection for him and the deepest regret for what had taken place between them, and that he had received from him a charge to tell him that he had withdrawn his curse and had prayed a blessing on him. The son receives the intelligence with grateful joy, and his burden drops from him. *He is saved by faith.* His mind is healed by believing the information that has been given him. His father's forgiveness is not given him as a reward of his believing this history—but unless he believes it, the forgiveness is quite useless to him—he will continue to feel his father's curse clinging to him. But let me now here suppose for a moment that the friend, instead of simply relating to him the fact of his father's forgiveness, had put the whole history into the form under which the gospel is very often preached. Suppose he had said to him, "Your father has forgiven you, if you believe in my testimony of his forgiveness, but if you cannot do this, there is no forgiveness for you." One can easily imagine the perplexity into which the son would be thrown by such an announcement. It would appear to him as if the truth of a past fact depended on the state of his feeling about it. It would be impossible for him in such circumstances to believe because his informant told him that his belief of the pardon must precede the existence of the pardon.

I have not here supposed the existence of any penalty or positive infliction attending the curse that might be removed by the forgiveness. I have considered it only as the means of relieving a mental distress. In this latter view, it is quite evident to common sense that faith in the forgiveness is necessary to give it any efficacy. But if there be positive inflictions or penalties to be removed by the pardon, this effect may be produced altogether independently of faith in the pardon. Thus, had the father disinherited his son and then cancelled the deed, the son's right of succession would not have been at all affected by his belief or unbelief of his father's forgiveness.

In like manner, had the evils under which man labors consisted merely in external penalties and judicial inflictions, his faith in the forgiveness that removed them would never have been required because his faith gives no efficacy to the pardon in this respect. But if a great part of the misery of sin consists in the diseased condition of the mind produced by it—if it consists mainly in the state of the thoughts and feelings, then a pardon that would deliver from this misery must address and enter the thoughts and feelings, that is to say, it must be understood and felt—and how can it be so unless it is believed?

The use of faith, then, is not to remove the penalty or to make the pardon better—for the penalty is removed and the pardon is proclaimed whether we believe it or not—but to give the pardon a moral influence by which it may heal the spiritual disease of the heart, which influence it cannot have in the nature of things unless it is believed. When a messenger from heaven made known to the shepherds of Bethlehem that the Savior was born and that through Him peace was proclaimed on earth and goodwill from God to man—the truth of the fact and the sincerity of that goodwill that the Creator thus manifested towards his creatures did not depend at all on the faith of the shepherds. But their own spiritual healing, as far as it was connected with joy and gratitude and hope, depended entirely on their belief of the message.

Men are not, according to the gospel system, pardoned on account of their belief of the pardon, but they are sanctified by a belief of the pardon. And unless the belief of it produces this effect, neither the pardon nor the belief is of any use. The use of a medicine is to restore health. If it does not accomplish this, it is useless. The pardon of the gospel is a spiritual medicine—faith is nothing more than the taking of that medicine, and if spiritual health or sanctification is not produced, neither the spiritual medicine nor the taking of the medicine are of any avail. They have failed in their object.

The gratuitousness of the gospel, then, consists in the unrestricted freeness of the pardon that it proclaims. Its terms are without condition and without exception. The form of its announcement is, "peace on *earth*, and good-will towards *men*."[13] It proceeded from that love with which God so loved the *world*, as to give His only begotten Son for it. And the Dispenser of the pardon said that he came to seek and to save the *lost*. It is to *sinners, as sinners*, that it is addressed, not to believing sinners, nor repenting sinners, nor amending sinners, but *to sinners*. But *pardon* is not *heaven*—heaven is not proclaimed to sinners. It belongs only to those who hate sin. Heaven is the joy of God, and we cannot enter the joy of God without entering into the character of God.

Why the Gospel Must Be Free

But it may be said, why is not the pardon reserved as a reward and an excitement of meritorious exertion instead of being lavished upon the

---

13. Luke 2:14, KJV.

mass of the guilty without any discrimination? The answer to this objection is that Christian obedience does not consist in doing certain actions and abstaining from others without regard to the motive from which this conduct proceeds—Christian obedience consists in holy love to God in habitual exercise. Now it is quite evident that no hope of reward whatever could produce *this obedience.* The heart cannot be bribed to love by anything except by the real or apparent amiableness of the object. A man, to be sure, might do or suffer many things to obtain pardon of sin, but this is not the obedience that the law of God requires. It requires the heart. It requires a generous, disinterested [that is free from selfish motive] love that longs to express itself in every possible act of devotedness and then counts all little and vile in comparison of the worthiness of Him whom it desires to please. The obedience that God asks is the free obedience of a child, not a mercenary negotiation for a deliverance from punishment. True obedience can only be paid by a spirit that rejoices that God requires its love, both because it recognizes in this demand a Father's heart, and because it feels that amidst all its failures and all its weaknesses, it yet has love to give. It is impossible that such a love as this can exist in a heart that feels the weight of unpardoned sin and that regards God as an offended governor and condemning judge. An assurance of forgiveness must precede confidence, and what love can there be without confidence? It is reasonable then to think that He who demands the love of the heart should begin by removing that fear of punishment that would prevent love.

But the gospel is much more than a pardon. What is the gospel? It is nothing and can be nothing other than a manifestation of God in relation to sinners. If our hearts were attracted to anything other than God, even though it were a pardon, we should still be out of our place in the spiritual system. For God is the center of that system and nothing but God. The pardon of the gospel, then, is just a manifestation of the character of God in relation to sinners. And that character is holy compassion. In relation to His sinless and happy creatures, His character is holy complacency, but in relation to those who are sinful and weak and miserable, it is holy compassion. This is at least the prominent feature in the manifestation, but it contains all. It is God in Christ reconciling the world unto Himself.[14] This pardon, then, is an unchangeable thing like God himself. Man, neither makes it nor merits it. God reveals it or rather reveals Himself in it. God, manifest in the flesh, becomes the representative of sinners. He

---

14. A reference to 2 Cor 5:18–19.

takes upon Himself their nature and the consequences of their rebellion that He might show Himself just even when justifying the ungodly, and that He might show himself gracious even when punishing sin.[15] His sufferings and death give the solemn and appalling measure of the divine condemnation of sin and of the divine compassion for the sinner.

When the Spirit of God reveals this to the heart, all self-pleasing thoughts of personal merit are extinguished. What have we done to Him or for Him who has done this for us? We have paid Him by preferring the least of His gifts before Himself—by turning a deaf ear to His condescending invitations of fatherly kindness and by offering Him the base and reluctant service of our hands and ceremonial [service] of our tongues as an adequate return for His heart's love. If we know this love, we shall feel annihilated by it—we have nothing to give in return that is not despicable when considered as a payment. But He asks no payment. He asks but the love of the spirit which He has made as that in which He delights—and as that in which the good and the happiness of the creature consists. He has dearly earned our gratitude and our confidence, and these feelings when worked into the heart, put us in our proper place towards God— affectionate dependence. Affectionate dependence on the Creator is the spiritual health of the creature, as averseness and independence are the spiritual disease of the creature.

The Nature of Sin

Men are very apt to consider sin as consisting merely in this or that particular action. The old philosophers taught that virtue was the mean between two extremes, thus the virtue of generosity is the mean between prodigality and avarice, courage the mean between rashness and timidity, and so of the rest. On this system, the difference between virtue and vice lay merely in the degree, not in the kind. But the word of God teaches another sort of morals. According to it, sin consists in the absence of the love of God from the heart as the dominant principle.[16] So, sin is not so much an action as a manner of existence. It is not necessary to go to the expense of an action in order to sin—the habitual state of most minds, of all minds indeed naturally, even in their most quiet form, is sin; that

15. Erskine is here giving us a glimpse into how he believes the representative sacrifice and atonement of Christ works.

16. Matt 22:37–40.

is to say, the love of God is not dominant in them. The centripetal force constitutes an element in every line in which the planet moves in its orbit. Were the influence of this force to be suspended, we should not think of reckoning the number of aberrations that the planet might make in its ungoverned career. We should say that its whole manner of being, severed from the solar influence, was a continued and radical aberration. In like manner, the soul ought to feel the love of God as a governing element along the whole course of its existence—every movement of thought and feeling and desire ought to contain it as an essential part of its nature. And when this principle is wanting, we need not count the moral aberrations that the spirit makes. Its whole existence is an aberration. It is an outlaw from the spiritual system of the universe. It has lost its gravitation.

In such a state of things, it is evident that a pardon that did not bring back the wanderer and restore his lost gravitation would be of no use to him. Until his gravitation is recovered, he is a blot on the creation. Love to God is the gravitation of the soul, and it is restored by the operation of the Spirit who takes of the things of Christ and shows them to the soul. Faith is the receiving of the Spirit's instruction. A faith that does not restore spiritual gravitation is useless, and that only is true gravitation that keeps the soul in its orbit.

The movement of the soul along the path of duty under the influence of holy love to God constitutes what are called good works. Good works are works that proceed from good principles. The external form of an action cannot alone determine whether it be a good work or not. Its usefulness to others may be determined by its external form, but its moral worth depends on the moral spring from which it flows. Good works, then, are properly healthy works or works of a healthy mind. Healthy bodily actions can only proceed from healthy bodily principles, and healthy spiritual actions can proceed only from healthy spiritual principles. A man who has lost his health does not recover it again by the performance of healthy bodily actions for of these his bad health renders him incapable, and in that incapacity, indeed, his bad health consists, but by the use of some remedial system and as health returns, its proper and natural actions return along with it. His health is not produced by these actions, but it is followed by them and strengthened by them.

The enjoyment of the body consists in these healthful actions. They are the spontaneous language of health. They constitute the music, as it were, that results from the organs being well tuned. It is the same thing with the actions of the soul. Spiritual health is not acquired by good actions. It is followed by them and strengthened by them. They also are music, sweet music. And oh, were these spirits of ours with their thousand strings but rightly tuned, what a swell of high and lovely song would issue from them—a song of holy joy and praise commencing even here and still rising upwards until it mixed with the full harmony of that choir which surrounds the throne of God. Good works, then, are not undervalued by those who hold the doctrine of *unconditional pardon* in its highest sense. On the contrary, they have a more elevated place in their system than in the system of those who regard them as the price paid for pardon. For, according to the *unconditional system*, good works are the perfection and expression of holy principles, the very end and object of all religion, the very substance of happiness, the very element of heaven. Whereas, on the *conditional system*, they are only the way to happiness, or rather, the price paid for it. There is surely more honor paid to them in making them the *end* than the *means*, the building than the scaffolding, and in attributing to them an intrinsic than a conventional value.

Good works are holiness in action—and this is a chief element of heaven. Some moralists have thought that the hope of heaven taints the purity of virtue by destroying its disinterestedness [not influenced by considerations of personal advantage]. But they do not know what heaven is. It is the sense of his spiritual corruption rather than the sense of sorrow that makes the Christian long after heaven. The holiness of heaven is still more attractive to him than its happiness. In heaven also the affections meet and are forever united to their proper object. They are filled and satisfied with the presence of God. It is this that they thirst after. They desire his favorable presence as their chief good. It is an interest undoubtedly—the highest interest, but is it a selfish interest? Shall the desire of a son to behold once more the face of his father after a few years of absence be esteemed a pure and generous desire, and shall the desire of a spirit long exiled from its native sphere to return to its Father and its God, the center of its being, the fountain light and life and love, be called a selfish or interested desire? No, it is a pure desire that is sent down into the spirit from the heart of God and that remains unsatisfied until it has again mingled with its source. No, it is a noble desire and speaks a noble origin. And the fear connected with the idea of missing this object is not a base fear—it is the horror that a pure spirit feels at the thought of mixing with pollution and of being tainted by it. The desire of doing that which is right for its own sake is in truth a part of the Christian's desire after heaven.

Forgiveness and Faith:
Essay II

The Representative Sacrifice of Christ

My Dear Friend,

Turn, if you please, to the Epistle to the Romans, 6th chapter, 1st verse. ["What shall we say then? Shall we continue in sin that grace may abound?"] I venture to think that the meaning of the apostle has been very generally mistaken by translators and commentators. Our version (and all the others agree with it) supposes him to be meeting an objection that might naturally be made to the moral tendency of his doctrine. He had just given a most magnificent view of the riches of divine grace, and he supposes that someone may say, "But does not this system lead to indulgence in sin? If our own "deservings" has nothing to do with our pardon, why not go on in our own way relying on the treasury of merit that is in Christ?" Doubtless, this is a most important point in the Christian scheme, but if we look attentively at the answer that is contained in the six following verses, we shall, I think, conclude that the apostle had some other meaning in the first verse than our version has attributed to him. The moral tendency of the doctrine of grace would have been his theme if he had intended to answer such an objection as that which is supposed. *But instead of this, we find in these verses only a most direct and explicit assertion of the substitution of Christ in the place of the guilty and of their virtual participation (in consequence of this substitution) in all that he has done or is doing as their representative.*[1] Allow me to give here a transla-

---

1. Emphasis added by the editor. In one sentence, Erskine has summarized Paul's main thought in Rom 6 and at the same time much of Christian theology. The Nicene Creed attests to the fact that Jesus Christ was "the only Son of God, eternally begotten

tion, perhaps a little free, but such as I am sure could be well defended of the following verses:

> Not so: how shall we who have already died under the condemnation of sin continue under it now that we are restored to life? (And we have in truth virtually both suffered death and been restored to life,) for do you not know that as many of us as were baptized into the doctrine of Christ Jesus[2] were baptized into the doctrine that he died as the representative of sinners.[3] We were thus virtually buried with him according to our baptismal acknowledgment of the nature of his death, and then, as Christ was raised from the dead by the power of the Father, we also walk in a life newly bestowed. For if we have been connected[4] with him by being ranked under his death, (or by virtual participation in his death,) we shall also be ranked under his resurrection. Knowing this that our old man was crucified in him as our representative, so that that part of us that was subject to condemnation has already suffered it, and thus we continue no longer under condemnation for he who has suffered the penalty of death, has exhausted the condemnation.[5]

of the Father; God from God, Light from Light, true God from true God." Only by being both fully God and fully human could He be humanity's representative and die in our stead. Jesus, the Messiah, did not deserve to suffer condemnation and death. Yet, He willingly became humanity's representative before God and died on behalf of all humankind. Only in this way could He become the atoning sacrifice for the sins of the whole world.

2. Gal 3:27—"For as many of you as have been baptized into Christ have put on Christ."

3. Hearkening back to Rom 5:6, 8. Christ "died on behalf of the ungodly" (v. 6, NTE). "The Anointed died on our behalf" (v. 8, DBH).

4. Or *united* as most modern translations translate Romans 6:5.

5. It has been suggested that Thomas Erskine helps us to understand the later writings of T. F. Torrance (1913–2007) and T. F. Torrance helps us to understand Thomas Erskine's. Here are a few lines from Torrance that suggest this to be true.

"Jesus was baptised with the baptism of repentance not for his own sake but for ours, and in him it was our humanity that was anointed by the Spirit and consecrated in sonship to the Father. . . . He received the baptism meant for sinners. In our human nature he received the divine judgment upon sin; in our human nature he made atonement, and in our human nature he rose again from the dead. When he was born, died, and rose again, it was in our human nature which was born and consecrated as the Messiah, and that he, the Righteous One, became one with us, taking upon himself our unrighteousness, that his righteousness might become ours. For us, baptism means that we become one with him, sharing his righteousness, and that we are sanctified in him as members of the messianic people of God, compacted together in one Body in Christ" (Torrance, *Theology in Reconciliation*, 86–87).

Now I would ask my candid man whether these verses contain the most distant solution of the difficulty supposed to be stated in the first verse. Their single object is to show that condemnation is perfectly exhausted and finished by the representative sacrifice of Christ. One would be led to infer from this that the question in the first verse refers not to the principle of sin, but to the continuing in a state of condemnation, which gives to *hamartia*[6] the same signification in this passage that it evidently bears through the preceding chapter. And this, I am very much persuaded, is the truth. "Shall we continue," not in sin, but "in a state of condemnation?"[7] But how is this to be reconciled with the last clause in the interrogation, "that grace may abound"? I think that both clauses have been wrongly translated. Observe that the word here translated "abound" is *pleonázō*,[8] not *pĕrissĕuō*.[9] This is of importance as I hope to prove to you. In the preceding chapter the apostle had been explaining the nature of the analogy that subsisted between Christ and Adam as the representative heads of their respective families. He had been speaking of the universality of the sentence of death that has fallen upon the descendants of Adam in consequence of their federal connection with him as illustrative of the universal restoration that is derived through Christ. Here then was *one great restoration* opposed to *one great forfeiture*,[10] both of them being perfectly independent of the deservings of those who were the subjects of them. But then, in the 20th verse, he says that a change was produced on this state of things by the introduction of the principle of *law* into the world. When men learned that they were bound to the fulfilment of certain duties that were attached to the various relations in which they stood towards God and towards man, and when they found that they sinned against these duties, their conscience told them that they had incurred a forfeiture by their own deserving, independent altogether of that original forfeiture that lay upon the whole race in consequence

6. Greek *hamartia* (Strong's 266) meaning "offense, sin".

7. *The New Testament for Everyone*, a translation by N. T. Wright, agrees with Erskine. That translation renders the question as, "Shall we continue in the state of sin, so that grace may increase?"

8. Greek *pleonázō* (Strong's 4121) meaning "to do, make or be more."

9. Greek *pĕrissĕuō* (Strong's 4052) meaning to "superabound (in quantity or quality)."

10. Erskine uses the word "forfeiture" repeatedly throughout this section. The concept is that in the fall, Adam forfeited the privilege of divine blessings (chief among them being eternal life as a son or daughter of God), but through Christ comes the restoration of the divine blessings that were lost.

of Adam's sin. Thus, by the introduction of law, instead of there being but *one* forfeiture extending overall, there resulted as many forfeitures as there were individuals who had broken the law. Every man had a forfeiture peculiar to himself distinct from that great forfeiture under which he lay in common with all the species. This increase of the number of forfeitures is expressed by the word *pleonázō* not *pěrissěuō*, both words, though used antithetically in the original, are translated by the same term "abound" in our version. "But law entered to the effect of increasing the number of forfeitures, but where the condemnation was thus *multiplied*, grace *abounded* over them all"[11] as oil out of one cask covers a pond nourished by a hundred springs. *Pleonázō* relates to number and variety; *pěrissěuō* relates to quantity and extension. In this 20th verse, *pěrissěuō* is the word used to express the extension of grace—it is *one* great grace extending over *many* forfeitures. Well, now look at the first verse of the 6th chapter and apply these remarks. The original word here translated *abound* is not *pěrissěuō* but *pleonázō*. It ought, therefore, according to this theory to be translated "multiplied."[12] It refers to *an increase of the number of the acts* of grace and not to the extension of the *one* great act over all forfeitures.[13] I think that the meaning is this: The apostle seems to have taken it for granted that the *one great restoration* through Christ met and remedied the *one great forfeiture* through Adam. But after he had spoken of the *personal* forfeiture that each individual has incurred for himself, he apprehended that they might think that some *personal* manifestation of pardon, something over and above that one great and general restoration, was necessary for each individual before he was warranted to look to or approach God as a propitiated God. Well says the apostle, "What shall we say? The one great forfeiture is no doubt remedied by the one great atonement, but will this one general restoration meet and remedy also the multiplied and varied forfeitures of individual deserving?" As long as there was but *one* forfeiture, it seemed reasonable that *one* restoration should suffice, but now that the forfeitures have been multiplied, may we not expect that there will be manifested a corresponding increase or multiplication of the acts of atonement? "Shall we continue under condemnation

11. Paraphrasing Rom 5:20.

12. The *New Revised Standard Version* lends its support to Erskine's translation. It renders Rom 5:20 as "But law came in, with the result that the trespass *multiplied*; but where sin increased grace *abounded* all the more."

13. The *Holman Christian Standard Bible* captures this nuance thus: "The law came along to multiply the trespass. But where sin multiplied, grace multiplied even more."

until grace be also multiplied, until the acts of atonement equal the number of the forfeitures? Not so, how shall we, who have already died under the sentence of sin, yet continue under it now that we are restored to life?" The fact, then, that we have already died under sin and now live, if proved, demonstrates that the sentence is exhausted and, of course, is no longer in force. He then gives an exposition of the representative character of Christ in relation to men as a proof of the fact. They acknowledged when they professed themselves Christians at baptism that his death was for theirs and that his resurrection involved theirs. He takes their own baptismal acknowledgment of the vicarious death and resurrection of Christ as a proof to them that the *one* atonement was as much a remedy for the *multiplied personal forfeitures* as for the *one general forfeiture*. All had already been done in the way of atonement that ever was to be done or that ever needed to be done. The access to God propitiated was open. The blood that had been shed cleansed from all sin. To every individual of the apostate family was it said, "Return unto me, for I have redeemed thee."[14] The pardon was universal and unconditional as far as it went for the proclamation was, "peace on earth and good will towards men"[15]— and it revealed "God in Christ reconciling *the world* unto himself not imputing unto them their trespasses";[16] and it bore that "the Son of God had been made a propitiation for the sins of the whole world."[17] The pardon of the gospel then is in effect a declaration on the part of God to every individual sinner in the whole world that His holy compassion embraces him, and that the blood of Jesus Christ has atoned for his sins. This is the declaration of God, and He makes it the ground of His urgent invitation to sinners to return to Him and walk with Him. This return to God and walking with God constitute the wellbeing of a creature, and without this,

14. An allusion to Isa 44:22. The full quote is: "I have blotted out, as a thick cloud, thy transgressions, and, as a cloud, thy sin; return unto me; for I have redeemed thee."

15. Erskine is here quoting the Christmas carol "I Heard the Bells on Christmas Day," which follows the Authorized Version's translation of Luke 2:14. Some modern translations read, "on earth peace to men on whom his favor rests." Which translation is better? Both have something to teach us. The Authorized Version more accurately reflects the prophecy found in Zech 9:9–10. "See, your king comes to you, righteous and having salvation, gentle and riding on a donkey, on a colt, the foal of a donkey. . . . He will proclaim peace [with God] to the nations" (NIV). The alternate translations remind us that peace with God only comes to those who receive him and allow his peace to rest on them.

16. 2 Cor 5:19.

17. 1 John 2:2.

the declarations of God's love are useless to the creature. God so loved the world (the whole world—all the race of Adam)[18] as to give his only begotten Son for them—but those only who believe this love, who receive it into their hearts, are saved by it. The love of God abiding in the heart and governing the will of the creature is its salvation—there is no other salvation than this, and therefore while the pardon that is the proclamation of God's love remains on the outside of the heart, while it does not enter in, it produces no salvation. The pardon therefore is not so much a particular act as a manifestation of God opening the inviting arms of His love to perishing sinners and urging them to come to Him that they may have life. There is no more exclusion. All are urged to come, and those who do come are transformed by the light of the glory of God and by His powerful Spirit that is given to those who come into His likeness, and in His likeness, the holiness and happiness, the heaven and eternal life of the creature consist. The validity of the pardon does not depend on man's believing or not. The pardon remains always the same—the access always remains open. The invitation is always urgent, but those who do not come in are not transformed.

This passage of Scripture, taken in the sense that I have attributed to it, appears to me most valuable. It lays the axe to the root of the whole system of supererogation,[19] whether called works or faith. It condemns that *theological* edifice in which faith as an act of man's mind occupies the place that the atonement of Christ holds in the *Bible* edifice. According to the common method of religious instruction amongst many truly serious persons, pardon is represented as so dependent on faith that it is apt to be mistaken for its reward, and then, as these teachers fear that this may appear to offer heaven on too easy terms, they attach to their definition of faith the whole Christian character in order as it would seem to make it more worthy of such a reward. If they would only distinguish in their systems, between pardon and salvation, the one being the spiritual *medicine*, the other the spiritual *cure*, they would find themselves much

18. The heart of the book is found in this paragraph. Erskine has here explicitly stated his belief that God loves all human beings, that Christ died for all, and therefore, the atonement of Christ must be universal. Many in the Church of Scotland at the time considered this heresy. In 1831, only three years after Erskine's book was published, the General Assembly of the Church of Scotland deposed John McLeod Campbell, minister of Row, for preaching the doctrine of "universal atonement and pardon through the death of Christ." By the end of the 1800s, the situation had changed, and the doctrine of limited atonement as previously understood had itself come under fire.

19. The act of performing more than is required by duty, obligation, or need.

more unembarrassed both in declaring the freeness of the gospel and the necessity of conformity to the law. For what is the freeness of the gospel upon their system but substituting faith as the ground of a sinner's hope in the place of obedience, which is called the legal system? When a man looks into his own mind to discover faith there as a ground of his hope before God, he is just wandering as wide from the gospel as the man who is counting his alms deeds for the same purpose, and he is wandering perhaps still more widely from present peace than the legalist because the man who counts his alms deeds has substantial matter to rest on such as it is, but faith is a state of mind that is not susceptible of definite proof, and when the spirit is depressed and is most anxious to find it, it will often seem to vanish. Sanctification is the true meaning of salvation,[20] and it is produced by faith in the atonement, but the atonement is itself the pardon and is unaffected by man's belief or unbelief. Some theologians have endeavored to [avoid][21] difficulties by supposing that the gospel consists of a testimony and a promise—a testimony that Christ died for sin and a promise that those who believe in this testimony shall be pardoned. But this is still confounding pardon and salvation and making pardon the recompense of faith. It appears to me that the testimony of the Bible is *that sinners* ARE *pardoned for Christ's sake*, and that the promise is that those who through this newly slain and living way approach to God will be sanctified and conformed in the spirit of their minds to the will of God, and this is heaven and salvation.

The Obstacle between God and Man Removed

The punishment of sin was exclusion from the favorable presence of God, and the gospel cancels this exclusion by declaring *peace on earth, and goodwill towards men*. On the great day of atonement in the Jewish church, previous to the sprinkling of the blood, the doors of the tabernacle were shut, and the people excluded from the emblems of the divine presence in representation of the desert of sinners. As soon, however, as the blood of the victim was sprinkled, the doors were opened, and the people invited to enter, the exclusion ceased. A Jew might, even after the

---

20. The Greek word translated "sanctification" (*hagiasmos*) means "holiness." To sanctify, therefore, means "to make holy." Erskine saw salvation in terms of its ultimate end, which he believed to be deliverance from sin itself and restoration to the image of God.

21. Replaced "get quit of."

opening of the doors, have remained without, and he would thus have missed those favors that God has promised to those who seek His face, but his exclusion was not judicial. It was voluntary. It was a sore evil to his soul but not a punishment. The transforming of his mind according to the will of God depended on his spiritual communion with God, and he excluded himself from the appointed way of obtaining this communion. But his refusal to enter did not shut the door, did not cancel the invitation, did not reverse the pardon. A pardon that did not bring him into the presence of God and subject him to the sanctifying influence of that presence was of no use to him—but it did not cease on that account to be a pardon. He made no use of it, but he might have made use of it. He was pardoned but not saved.

His entrance into the tabernacle, the type of spiritual communion with God, was the object for which the blood was sprinkled, and the doors opened—but he had slighted the privilege and had thus strengthened his own dislike to the purity of the divine presence. He was spiritually in a worse condition than he was before, but still the door was open, and the blood retained its power, and the pardon continued in force.

Nothing but spiritual communion with God as the God of holy love can sanctify the soul. And nothing but a conviction of God's kindly disposition towards sinners will ever lead a sinner into the presence of God. While conscience declares condemnation, she acts the part of the cherubim who kept back man from the tree of life. She forbids that spiritual communion that is the only remedy for fallen nature. The Apostle, therefore, is most minute and explicit as well as most urgent in declaring this most precious truth that all is already done in the way of atonement which guilt on the one side can possibly require or unlimited mercy on the other side can devise. No obstacle whatever remains between God and man. The blood of the everlasting covenant—that blood that cleanses from all sin, has been shed and sprinkled. The doors that barred the favorable presence of God from the guilty have been thrown wide—God is there seated on a throne of mercy waiting to hear and answer prayer, inviting us to come in and to go no more out, to hold spiritual communion with him, and to be his sons and daughters. What is our warrant to accept of this invitation? Can it be anything other than the invitation itself? Nothing surely. *Our belief of the invitation is no warrant.* If the invitation is a good and true invitation, our belief of it cannot make it better or truer. And if it is a false invitation, our belief of it cannot make it good or true. The Bible says that the door is open. Let us then enter.

Already Forgiven

There are many, however, who are perplexed and injured exceedingly in their spiritual interests by this very doubt. They say, we fear that we have not that faith in Christ that warrants us to go confidently to God in his name. I would answer these persons, in the words of the Apostle: "Shall we continue under the sentence of exclusion from the divine presence, until a special atonement has been made for each of us?" Is the one great atonement insufficient? What do you wait for? There remains no further sacrifice for sin.[22] When you read that men are saved by faith, it does not mean that they are pardoned on account of their faith or by their faith. No, its meaning is far different. It means that they are pardoned already before they thought of it, that the sentence of exclusion has been reversed, and that the belief of this kindness will and ought to carry them directly in gratitude and in hope into the presence of that kind Father who is waiting to be gracious to them and to treat them as His children.

The reversal of the sentence of exclusion that I here consider to be pardon is universal. Those who do not feel the preciousness of this restoration, and who are not touched by the holy love that planned and executed it, remain, of course, unbenefited by it. Their spiritual corruption is their great evil, and the good news of a propitiation was made known to them simply for the purpose of healing this corruption—but they have neglected the remedy, and therefore, the cure is not performed. They are still diseased and miserable, enemies to God and to their own souls. But yet, in spite of all this, the door continues open for them, and the invitation continues urgent, and the spiritual medicine that is preferred to them in the pardon still retains all its healing virtue. They will not come that they may be healed.

I have sometimes been led to think that justification often is used to signify *not pardon, but a sense of pardon*, and that therefore, it is so much connected with faith. "Being justified by faith, we have peace with God."[23] It is not a pardon simply, but a pardon known and believed that will give peace. But then, though our belief of the pardon gives us peace, yet it does not make the pardon one iota better than it was before. This sense of pardon, however, is the only thing that can lead us into the presence of God with childlike confidence. It is the only thing that can enable us to look at the justice and holiness of God without dislike and fear. It is

22. Heb 10:12.

23. Rom 5:1.

the only thing that can produce holy gratitude, and the greatness of the gratitude will be in proportion to the sense entertained of the greatness of the pardon. The two debtors mentioned in the concluding passage of the 7th chapter of Luke were both forgiven, but the one had the sense of great forgiveness, the other of a small one, and their gratitude was in direct proportion to their sense of forgiveness. Let us suppose that both owed five hundred pence, and that both were freely forgiven, but that one knew the amount of his debt while the other did not know that he was a debtor at all. The one would feel gratitude for his forgiveness. The other would have no sense of forgiveness at all, and therefore, no gratitude. I conceive all men to be in this state, that all are forgiven—but that those only who know somewhat of the amount of their debt and the value of that ransom by which they were redeemed, love Him who has thus loved them—the rest, those who are ignorant that they have incurred a condemnation cannot appreciate the love of Him that pitied them, and therefore, they love Him not. But heaven and happiness and salvation are all summed up in Holy Love—and it was to produce holy love that the atonement of Christ was proclaimed. If the proclamation has not produced holy love, it has produced neither heaven nor happiness nor salvation. Hence arises the necessity of the knowledge of duty in all its extent in order to appreciate the value of redemption. We cannot love much until we know that we are forgiven much, and we cannot know that we are forgiven much, until we know what the law of God requires from us.

It may appear to some at first sight that this system is calculated to give false peace and to set the whole world at their ease, but this is an unfounded apprehension. The prominent part of the system is that the two great commandments describe *heaven* as well as duty, and that an opposition to them in the heart is *hell* as well as disobedience. On these two commandments hang all the law and the prophets, and the gospel too. The law and the prophets and the gospel have been sent for the purpose of writing these two commandments in the heart. And until they are written there, heaven is not there, nor salvation. Do we love God? Do our thoughts, our desires, our words, our actions, refer to Him and tend to Him? Do we love our neighbor for the sake of Him who has made him and redeemed him and commanded us to love him? If we do, we are in possession of salvation, and if we do not, conscience must declare that we are not in possession of it. Oh! What a continual call is here to the blood of sprinkling, both to satisfy the conscience and to excite the heart—to calm agitations and passions and apprehensions and to give renewed confidence in the willingness and faithfulness of God to bestow His living Spirit to sanctify us and to do for us exceedingly above all that we can ask or think.

The gospel explains that great commandment and contains the dynamics by which its behests may be obeyed. Who, it may be asked, is this God whom we are called on thus to love? It is that God who has so hated sin and so loved the world that He gave His only begotten Son to the death to condemn sin and to save the world. This is the God whom we are called on thus to love. That blood-branded sin—it removed every obstacle that barred the approach of the sinner to God or of God to the sinner, and it gave a pledge and a specimen of the richness and the holiness of divine love. This revelation is the instrument by which the Spirit of God writes the law upon the heart in fulfilment of the promise made through Jeremiah 31:33.[24] It was given that men might see God as He is and learn to love Him as He ought to be loved.

An unholy God may he approached familiarly and even, perhaps, in some degree loved by an impenitent sinner, but the God who so loved the world as to give His Son to expiate sin is a holy God. He takes no pleasure in wickedness. Those only can love Him who love purity.

The law is thus preached in perfect harmony with the unconditional freeness of the gospel. The fulfilment of the law is not the way to heaven. It is itself heaven. God is love. He who dwells in love dwells in God, and God in him. It is not a condition of salvation. It is itself salvation. The law contains the description of spiritual health. It is the description of that character that is alone capable of spiritual enjoyment. This character must be obtained before heaven is obtained in its true meaning. The history of God's holy love manifested in Christ when received into the heart is the seed of this character. It must be sown by the Spirit and watered by the Spirit. What shall we say to this? He will give the Holy Spirit to those who ask Him. And all are warranted and invited to ask. And shall we delay asking?

When eternity is before us and near us, shall we wait for any better warrant than the blood of Christ or any stronger assurance than the promise of God? Shall we continue under the sentence of exclusion from His presence until some change be wrought on our own mind in addition to the atonement of Christ? No, all the satisfaction for sin that the justice

---

24. Jer 31:33—"But this is the covenant that I will make with the house of Israel after those days, says the LORD: I will put My law in their minds, and write it on their hearts; and I will be their God, and they shall be My people" (NKJV).

of God requires has been made already. The way is open, and the voice of God assures all who come that they will in no way be cast out.

It may be objected to this view that it is opposed to all the scriptural examples of prayer that contain a petition for the pardon of sin. If sin is already pardoned, what is the use or meaning of continuing to ask pardon day by day or indeed at all? I think that the pardon that is asked is a sense of pardon, a sense of the divine nearness and love and not a special repeal of the sentence of exclusion that I conceive to be contained in the primary and universal proclamation of Christ to the world.[25] Is it conceivable that a spirit that ventures to address God by the appellation "Our Father" can really be asking the repeal of a sentence of everlasting banishment? The asking and the bestowing of pardon form a most interesting part of that endearing reciprocation of kindness that belongs to the relation of parent and child. "And if we know that He hears us, we know that we have the petitions which we ask,"[26] says the beloved disciple. These prayers are the expressions of humility and compunction and confidence, not the deprecations of wrath. And though a man has hitherto known nothing of this high and blessed relationship, yet the moment that he understands that God so loved sinners as to give His Son for them to take away their condemnation, he must and will have confidence that now there is no condemnation, no exclusion, and he will approach God with confidence. But though he does approach with confidence, he will yet confess sin and ask pardon for sin, and he will do so with the very feeling that filled the poor prodigal's heart when he made his confession with his father's arms around him, and his words of peace and welcome sounding in his ears.

The natural effect of every sin is to banish man from the presence of God. The sense of exclusion, more or less strong, must accompany every sin. The only remedy here, the only answer to conscience is the testimony of God that a victim has been slain whose blood cleanses from all sin. This is the only remedy, but it is quite sufficient. That testimony contains abundant assurance that the returning sinner will be well received. *The sense of pardon*, however, is necessarily connected with a present conviction of the truth of that testimony, and when the heart is wandering

---

25. Another answer that I find most satisfying and implied in Erskine's is that our asking is like a participation in the fact of forgiveness. We ask knowing that Christ *has* forgiven us and that we are sharing in His finished work, so after asking, we should always thank Him for His forgiveness. (Taken from a conversation between David W. Torrance and J. Michael Feazell.)

26. 1 John 5:15.

from God, it is wandering also from that testimony, and thus the sentiment of exclusion accompanies the sense of sin, and the renewed sense of pardon is accompanied with renewed convictions of the holiness and the mercy of God that counteract the danger of false peace. Will we then consider ourselves either honoring God or caring for our own spiritual progress while we continue outside the gate of the tabernacle doubting the sincerity of God's most unconfined and unconditional invitations to all to come in and waiting for some special act of grace in our own favor? Not so. How can we, who have in the person of our representative paid the penalty, yet continue under it? How can we, who are partakers in the life of that great one over whom death has no longer dominion, yet lie under the terror of condemnation? No, let us rather join in that song that Isaiah's prophetic ear heard though far away, "Oh LORD, I will praise Thee: though Thou wast angry with me, Thine anger is turned away, and thou hast comforted me."[27]

A universal amnesty is the subject of the divine testimony. A sense of pardon or justification belongs to those who believe the testimony, and the use of this sense of pardon is to write the love and law of God upon the heart. If it does not affect this, it has failed for that love and that law are salvation. Pardon is entirely irrespective of all the varieties of human character. *It belongs to man as a sinner. Heaven, on the contrary, consists in character.* This appears to me to be the scriptural doctrine of justification by faith, and up to this point, all is intelligible. A sinner is by judicial sentence excluded from the favorable presence of God, and he is spiritually diseased in consequence of his distance from God. The universal repeal of the sentence of exclusion on the ground of the death of Christ as the substitute of sinners is the message conveyed from God to man through the gospel. But although the exclusion is done away, man will yet keep at a distance from God until he knows who God is and what need he has of God, and that he will be made welcome by God, and while he continues at a distance from God, he continues unsaved. It is faith in the atonement and in what it signifies that heals the spiritual disease that saves the soul. The limitation then is not in the pardon but in the belief of the pardon. All are pardoned, but believers are a little flock. Why is this? This is the great mystery in religion. Here we pass into the infinite and are lost. One is taken and another left. One heart is made to hear the voice of God and learns from that teaching voice what flesh and blood cannot

27. Isa 12:1

reveal. Another reads the Bible and hears sermons and goes through the forms of prayer and seems even to long after spiritual religion, and yet he continues a stranger to spiritual communion with God. What is the meaning of this? God is the great king in all the earth. He does what pleases Him. He has promised the Holy Spirit to them that ask Him, and yet the very disposition to ask Him is His own gift. But the language of the Bible in inviting sinners to God is so free that we must either suppose that there is a deception in the Bible, or we must suppose that every man has the power of coming to God if he chooses. Let us bow before Him whose thoughts, although above our thoughts, and whose ways, although above our ways, are yet thoughts and ways of everlasting love towards our fallen race. We are of yesterday and know nothing. Let us look unto Him, and He will save us. The way is open.

Forgiveness and Faith: Essay III

The Spirit of Independence

IT is impossible to look into the Bible with the most ordinary attention without feeling that we have entered into a moral atmosphere quite different from that which we breathe in the world and in which the world lives. In the Bible, God is represented as doing everything and as being the cause and the end of everything. And man appears merely as he stands related to God, as either a mutinous creature or the subject of divine grace. Whereas in the world, and in the books that contain the history of the world, according to the world's judgment, man appears to do everything, and there is as little reference made to God as if there was no such being in the universe. "The fool hath said in his heart, there is no God, and we'll have none. Our lips are our own. We are they that ought to speak. Who is Lord over us?"[1] There seems to be a general conspiracy to shut God out of the world that he has made and to suppress all reports of His claims and rights and sovereign power. The old serpent deceived our race and poisoned it in its root by that well-chosen temptation that seduced our first parents, "ye shall be as gods."[2] He seems to have spoken the word into their very souls so that it became a part of their being, a part of their nature that they have transmitted to their posterity. All would be gods. And men live in this lie and strengthen each other in it, and they die in it.

1. A reference to Pss 14:1 and 53:1.
2. Gen 3:5.

Nothing seems more evident even to reason than that a creature can have nothing but what it receives from its Creator. But the pride of man's heart revolts at the idea of being only a receiver. Alas! This pride is his foolishness for it has separated him from the ever full and ever flowing fountain of divine love. He was formed a happy member of the happy family of God. All the members of that family are closely united unto God. He is their Creator and their Fountain, their Head, their Heart. Their lifeblood is the Holy Spirit of God flowing freely and fully through them. They are all receivers, but they are receivers of God, receivers of the love and holiness and joy of God. He is their strength to will and to do. In His light they see light, and in His glory, they are glorious. He is their full, satisfying, eternal portion abiding in them and they in Him. He feeds them with the hidden manna and gives them to drink of the water of life. He is also the bond that unites all the members of the family to each other, and there is no schism in that body. They all have their place in Him, and they are all one in Him and with Him. They are all dependent, but it is this very Spirit of dependence that keeps open all the sluices and avenues of their souls to admit the fullness of God. Each is a distinct individual, conscious of his own peculiar duties and peculiar blessedness, but the principle that unites him to God is stronger than the principle of separate individuality. He is more a member of God's family than an individual, and as this principle uniting him to God is stronger than the principle of his own individuality, he sees and judges and feels things in the light of God and as they relate to Him rather than in his own light or as they relate to himself individually. He is a sharer in the common light and common interests of the family. There is not a holy feeling in the universe that does not vibrate to his heart. He enters into the joy of his Lord and that embraces all joys.

We look at this picture from a distance and wonder at the madness of man that banished him from so fair a scene—but we need go no further than our own hearts to see the cause of this sad banishment. The spirit of dependence is wanting—that open door by which God enters the heart. The spirit of independence is the spirit of this world. It is what the world cherishes and admires, and it is what shuts the heart against God and cuts off its supply from the Fountain of Life. "Open thy mouth wide and I will fill it,"[3] says our God—is not His yoke indeed easy, and His burden light?—the yoke and burden of a boundless beneficence—"but My

---

3. Ps 81:10.

people would not hear My voice, Israel would none of Me."[4] They refused to receive their God. Oh, what a mass of misery was before the mind of our God when he uttered these words. They are few and simple, but they describe a madness and an iniquity and a sorrow passing utterance—but they also breathe compassion, and in that lies our hope for it is the compassion of God. As the approving love of God is the light and air and joy of His unfallen family, so His tender mercies, His long-suffering, His holy compassion manifested in Christ Jesus are the only hope of return to those who are fallen. But as His approving love enters the hearts of his happy children by no other avenue but at the open door of their dependence, even so must His holy compassion enter our hearts. It can enter at no other door. This is the gate of the Lord, the *Porta Santa* through which alone He enters. We may have much *knowledge* of religion without the spirit of dependence, but we can have none of the thing itself. And it is, perhaps, one of the chief snares and deceptions of our day to mistake the knowledge of religion for religion itself, and to receive the doctrines of Christianity without receiving the God revealed in the doctrines. We may pride ourselves on our knowledge of religion as upon any other knowledge, and thus we may be strengthening the spirit of independence and so barring the door of our hearts more securely against God while we are fondly flattering ourselves that we are opening to receive him. Oh, Lord, teach us your truth. Lead us in your ways.

Humility is another name for the spirit of dependence. It is the feeling of our true condition before God and of our relation to him. The world does not know what humility means. The world's humility is mere diffidence and fear—but true humility is confidence and assured hope for the truly humble heart recognizes itself as a mere receiver and feels that it is not its duty only, but its high privilege to be a receiver. It hears its Lord's voice saying open thy mouth wide and I will fill it. It opens and receives the fullness of the blessing. "For thus saith the High and Lofty One, Who inhabiteth eternity, I dwell in the high and holy place, with him also that is of a humble and contrite heart, to revive the spirit of the humble, and to revive the heart of the contrite ones."[5] Humility is another name for spiritual order. It teaches the branch to abide in the vine and to open its veins to receive the sap of the root. It subordinates the principle of private individuality to that principle that unites the creature to God, and thus it

---

4. Ps 81:11.

5. Isa 57:15.

restores the disordered hierarchy in the heart by replacing God upon his throne there. Humility is nothing but truth, and independence is nothing but a lie for it honors the branch above the vine and the member above the body and the creature above the Creator. It calls a stream a fountain, and a planet a sun.

It is impossible that the creature can perform a single spiritual act while it continues in the spirit of independence. The branch torn from the tree ceases to have its vegetable life and is no longer capable of performing the functions of that life because the sap of the root no longer circulates through it. And man torn from the spiritual system loses his spiritual life and his capacity of spiritual actions for the lifeblood of that system, even the Holy Spirit, no longer animates him. But still, as if impelled by the uneradicated instincts of his original nature formed for the exercise and enjoyment of spiritual life, he often desires and attempts to perform the functions of that life, not considering that he has separated himself from the source that alone supplies life and strength for the performance of these functions. No one wonders that a hand separated from the strength of the body by dislocation or fracture should be incapable of doing any service to the body. All the efforts of a hand in these circumstances are useless. The only reasonable hope lies in using means for curing the dislocation or fracture. Even so, the only hope for man lies in reunion with God by being grafted onto the true vine through the spirit of dependence. Nothing done by his own independent efforts can have the nature of a spiritual action. It is out of the spiritual system, and, therefore, it is why the Bible relates more to what God has done for grafting man again into the vine than to what he requires from man as duty. "I will run the way of Thy commandments, when Thou hast enlarged my heart"[6]—when You have delivered me from the narrowness of my own selfish individuality and grafted me on the root of Your own infinite love and quickened me by Your free Spirit and expanded my heart to embrace Your boundless will.

Man, assuredly, even in his fallen state retains those capacities that were originally given him for communion with the spiritual system, but while he remains unrenewed by the Spirit of God, they remain unexercised or at least unexercised in their right direction. They were originally destined to convey the water of life to the soul of man, but other waters have been sought out, and this pure heavenly stream has been rejected,

6. Ps 119:32.

and the noble aqueduct has fallen into decay. Their use was to connect him with the universality of the spiritual system, and they constituted the dominant part of his nature. While they were in healthful exercise, he saw things in the broad light of God's will and in their relation to the whole spiritual system. But now that he seeks to be independent and those capacities that connected him with the universal system are unexercised, his selfishness has taken the place of God in his heart, and he sees things in the light of his own will and in relation to his own individuality. The dominancy of this private will is the spirit of independence. It is this that bars the heart against God and heaven and makes each man the center of his own system. And thus, it is that when the natural man thinks of God, he regards Him merely in relation to his personal and private interest. He remains still the center of his own system, and it is a matter of interested [influenced by personal or selfish motives] consideration with him how much he should sacrifice to the will of God in order to secure himself from the consequences of his displeasure. This negotiation has nothing of religion in it. There is nothing in common between such feelings and the generous uncalculating devotedness of a child of God. It is from taking this view of religion that many philosophers have regarded it as a mere variety of the selfish system of morals. They consider heaven and hell as the great motives in Christianity, and these they regard only as rewards and punishments addressed to the interested feelings of selfish hope and fear. But this has nothing to do with religion. Selfish hope or fear may drive a man to seek after religion, but religion itself is another thing—it is the displacing of this selfish individuality from its supremacy in the heart and restoring that supremacy to Him whose right it is.

The moral reformations which men make on themselves uninfluenced by the Spirit of God are all the results of a wise and refined selfishness. They give up certain gratifications because they perceive that the pain of them overbalances their pleasure in this world or will overbalance it in the next. They do not wish to lose either their own good opinion or the opinion of their fellow creatures, or they submit to necessity. And thus, the doctrine of self-denial is foolishness to them. They say, show us that certain privations are good for our health or our reputation or our safety, and we shall feel it to be our wisdom to deny ourselves. But the idea of putting down self as self is unintelligible. Yet the fall of man consists in self having taken the place of God in the heart, and the object of the Christian duty of self-denial is not merely to pay homage to God but to weaken this usurper in our hearts and to unbar that door that shuts God out.

This will teach us to form a true view of God's purpose in making the life of man so full of sorrow. The greatest blessing that man can receive is to have his private individual will subordinated to the sentiment of his relationship with God. And yet his continual business in this world is to strengthen this individual will that opposes the entrance of God into his heart. He seeks its gratification in all things and is ever guarding against anything that may cross it. He thus blindly loves and feeds his disease and resists all the attempts of divine love to cure it. This is man's way, and it is a way that leads down to death. God's way is to cross [thwart] man's way that he may be turned from it and live. He crosses him in his good opinion of himself, in his confidence in his own strength, and in his own wisdom. He crosses him in his favorite schemes of happiness. He sends affliction after affliction. He pours bitterness into his soul. He sends disease and death into the circle of his friends. He gives him up to the idolatry of the creature and then tears his idol from him or makes it a curse to him. He lays him on a bed of sickness and tries him with pain and restlessness and brings him to the boundary that separates time from eternity and makes him look backwards into past time and forwards into the future eternity and shows him that he was made to dwell with God through eternity, and yet that all his past days have been spent in *unfitting* himself for this state, and he says to him, "how can thy heart endure or thy hands be strong on the day that I plead with thee."[7] Turn unto me, the only strength of the creature. This is the way of God towards man, of that God whose name is Love, and this is the way that He expresses His Love. It is thus that He shakes the bulwarks of independence that guard the entrance of the soul against God. It is thus that He convinces man of his guilt and weakness and ignorance and misery and persuades him to open the door of his heart to God and to take shelter under His compassionate omnipotence. Blessed are they who are persuaded. Blessed are they in whose hearts God makes a place for Himself, though it be by casting out all other joys.

But sorrow itself cannot break the selfishness of the heart. Sorrow is as selfish as joy. Its language sounds more like religion than that of joy, but in spirit, they are alike. Sorrow looks at the future because the present is painful. It looks to heaven because earth is painful, and it wishes that God or any other being who can, would deliver it from its pain. This is still self. It is Pharaoh trembling under the rod of Moses. It is still man

7. Ezek 22:14.

growing out of his own root and seeing things in his own light. And so, we often find that when the pain is removed, the religion is removed along with it. "When He smote them, they sought Him—but within a while, they forgot his works, and would none of His counsel."[8] When Pharaoh saw that there was a respite, he hardened his heart. Sorrow cannot take man off his own root and graft him on the true vine. But there is a great use in sorrow. It gives pause to the soul. It shows us that we are not able of ourselves to help ourselves and that the creature cannot satisfy us. It acquaints us with the fact that God's way is different from our way and presses us to inquire into the cause of this difference, and above all, it gives the thought of prayer because it gives the feeling of want, and thus by the divine blessing, it often becomes the instrument of drawing wandering perishing sinners back to God.

I have sometimes been led to think that in our modern systems of religion, the relationship between the Creator and the creature is too little regarded and too much [sub]merged in the particular doctrines of Christianity. No doubt it may be answered that this relationship is supposed and taken for granted in all religions—but this is not enough. The creative and sovereign and personal omnipotence of God is to our minds the subjective basis of deity, and the sentiment of creaturely dependence on Him that rises out of it and corresponds to it is the basis of religion in the creature. All the doctrines of Christianity are but the expressions of the character of the omnipotent Creator. They are His modes of acting, but He himself is the great thing. Without the sense of His living reality and the sentiment of relation to Him, there is no religion, and Christianity becomes a mere set of notions. There can be no doubt that a great deal of the Christianity of the world is of this spurious kind or at least has a mixture of it. And there are times in which God, by His dealings with us, sends a fearful conviction of it into the heart. He brings a genuine reality such as death and sets it before us and makes us feel how mere notions melt into nothing at its presence, and that no religion is of any value that does not unite us to God by a bond as real as death is real. The living personality of God, if I may use the expression, must animate and fill out the doctrines—otherwise they only tend to add a fatal security to the sleep of the soul. They may be subjects of talk to us as the gods of gold and silver furnished talk to Belshazzar and his lords until some providence surprise us as the handwriting on the wall surprised them and make us

8. Alluding to Pss 78:34 and 106:13.

feel and know what it is to be in the presence of the real God, whom we have not glorified.

I feel persuaded that no idea of a power external to us, however great, can ever produce the sentiment of creaturely dependence on the heart. There must be the sense of God within us as the root and basis of our being, as the continual supplier of strength for thought and action and the fountain from which our current runs or else dries up. The Bible is full of this feeling of God, subjective as well as objective. He is there not only the light that the eye sees, but He is the power of the eye to see the light.

It is a truth that ought to produce much watchfulness and self-distrust that practical atheism may enter into the profession of religion and may even become a zealous partisan of orthodox Christianity. It is the God who is revealed and contained in the doctrines that alarms and assails the independence of the natural man. When they are separated from Him and His omnipotence, when they become mere syllogisms or emblazonments, they can take their place under the dark shadow of the atheism of the heart as well as the syllogisms or emblazonments of any other science. How different are these *forms* from the overawing reality with which the doctrines are animated in the Bible. And Oh, how different is the effect produced by them on the hearts of their partisans from those cries and breathings of the creature after the Creator that are embalmed in the sacred record and that still seem to ascend to heaven like incense from an altar. "Thy hands have made me, and fashioned me, give me understanding, that I may keep Thy commandments."[9] "I will abide in Thy tabernacle for ever: I will trust in the covert of thy wings."[10] "I am Thine, Oh save me."[11] Happy spirit, you have found your fountain. Your cry enters with acceptance into the ears of the Lord of Sabaoth. "When Thou saidst unto me, seek My face, my heart said unto Thee, Thy face Lord will I seek."[12] Surely this sweet communion between heaven and earth is true religion. Oh, for the putting forth of that power that made the deaf to hear and the dumb to speak that such sounds might enter our hearts and draw forth such answers. To a spirit thus bound by a real bond to the real God, life and death are equal for it finds the will of God

---

9. Ps 119:73.

10. Ps 61:4.

11. Ps 119:94.

12. Ps 27:8.

in either, and His will is its delight. It finds God in everything, and God is its portion. When Jesus says, "Behold I come quickly," it answers, "Even so come, Lord Jesus."[13] This is to walk with God.

There is something inexpressibly mysterious and solemn in the relation of the creature to the Creator. There is no parallel to it in the universe. When I think of it, I am overwhelmed by it. I cannot conceive how I have the consciousness of a separate existence distinct from my Creator. It seems to me that I am in relation to Him as a ray of light to the sun, proceeding continually out of His substance and having no individuality of my own. We are apt to lower our idea of this relationship by comparing it to the relationship between men and their works. The potter forms the clay into a vessel, and that vessel is then completely independent of him—it does not require his thought or power to uphold its existence. And so, we are prone to think of God and His works as if they could exist independently of Him. But there is a vast difference. The potter takes advantage of the laws of nature that are in continual action independently of him—they uphold his work after it is finished as it was by the application of their power that he fashioned it. Thus, in fact, the potter does nothing as a creator. He only changes the position of the clay. But the laws of nature are the continual actings of God. There is no power in the universe but His, and where His power is, there is He. He made the clay and sustains it with its qualities and in whatever form it may be. The cessation of His *will* that it should exist would be the cessation of its existence. The uninterrupted actings of that will are the laws of nature, and in every one of these actings is the entire Godhead. The course of nature, the elements, the order of events, the existence and movement of all matter are the direct actings of God. And are not the existence and movement of mind, too, His actings? Surely it is so and must be so, but yet I feel that my will works contrary to His. My *will* is the sustained creature of His *will* from moment to moment, incapable of a single act without power communicated from Him—and yet I am conscious that it works contrary to Him and is morally responsible for so doing. This is too wonderful for me. I cannot comprehend it.[14] You have assailed me from all sides and laid your hand upon me.

With what feelings ought I to regard Him to whose infinite mind my individual existence with every particular of my history through the

13. Rev 22:20.

14. An allusion to Job 42:3.

future eternity has been from all past eternity a distinct and familiar idea. It was a birth of His mind from all eternity. At length He gave reality to it by calling me into life and giving me a substantial existence, and He has ever since sustained this life by His continually pervading presence on every part of my soul and body. I have never been a single moment separated from Him. It is impossible that I should be separated from Him without ceasing to exist. I have never been alone, and I know that through eternity I never will be alone.

I am sure that I have never formed a thought nor uttered a word nor done a deed where He has not been most intimately present, and where He has not been himself the acting power enabling me to think and speak and do. And here is the great marvel. I am conscious that these thoughts and words and deeds have been full of sin, and yet my conscience acquits Him and lays the undivided blame upon myself. Who can solve this difficulty?

What an unspeakable relationship this is! And what an infinite possibility of enjoyment rises out of this perpetually pervading presence seeing it is a presence of infinite holiness and love and beauty and wisdom! But it seems as if He were too near me to see Him as the eye sees not itself. Yet I feel assured that until I see Him and feel Him in his perpetually pervading presence of infinite holiness and love and beauty and wisdom, I cannot have that good for which I was created. This presence is my real home and my real portion, and until I become keenly aware of it, I am without a home and without a portion in the universe.

It is appalling to know that there is a Being so near me, surrounding me, and inhabiting me, and yet that He should remain unseen and unknown by me, and is it not still more dreadful to know that in this Being and His relationship with me is treasured up a possibility of good beyond utterance and beyond conception, and yet that I should have no part in it? Alas! that I should have a sense that informs me of the presence of material light and makes it a pleasant thing for me to behold the sun, and that I should have no sense to inform me of the presence of the Light of Life and to give me joy in conversing with His brightness.

At first sight it appears remarkable that the Bible should at the same moment charge men with the guilt of idolatry and of atheism. It would seem impossible that the same individual should be guilty of both. Atheism consists in having no God, and idolatry seems to consist in having too many. But in fact, there is no god in idolatry any more than in atheism. The notion of various independent powers, which is the spirit of idolatry, is also the spirit of atheism. God is the one power and the one Fountain that does all things and from which all things flow. The course of nature, the course of providence, the course of life and being are the actings of that power and streams from that fountain. The spirit of religion goes directly to this first cause and sees it and acknowledges it and feels it in all things. It regards second causes, whether they be the elements of nature or the actions of men as mere channels through which this first and only cause operates. It stops not at them. It regards life as a holy thing flowing out of this Fountain and returning thither. It lives and moves and has its being in God by the spirit of its will as well as by the necessity of its nature.[15] Atheism and idolatry both stop at second causes. They see independent powers in everything, and they are themselves independent. They acknowledge that there are powers superior to their own as one man is stronger than another. But they regard their existence as their own property though liable to be invaded and affected by superior powers, and on this property, they can stand and parley and make conditions with these powers whatever they may be. The spirit of dependence is the spirit of religion, and the spirit of independence is the spirit of atheism and of idolatry.

This atheism of the heart, then, this insensibility to God, this blindness to His direct actings, this spirit of independence under the influence of which we live surrounded by God and sustained by Him and yet entirely unconnected with Him in spirit and desire—this being the evil to be remedied by Christianity, does it not seem most reasonable to expect that there should be in the remedy a special putting forth of the direct agency of God, and that He should reveal himself through it in such a way that the soul may know and feel that it is God of a truth that works and none other than He? The branch separated from the vine cannot graft itself on again. If it could, the order of nature would be subverted. And man, separated from God, cannot according to the order of a higher nature again unite himself to God. Indeed, this appeals to me so full of the highest reason and evidence that I should consider the great purpose of Christianity absolutely defeated were it possible for man to become a Christian by his own unassisted efforts or without a conviction of the necessity of divine assistance. Nay, it would be an absurdity. It would be teaching the spirit of dependence by an argument for independence. It would be leading man to repose his all on God by showing Him that he

---

15. Acts 17:28.

could do without God. The true state of the creature is a state of absolute dependence on the Creator, and when he has left his true state, he can only be brought back to it by a way of absolute dependence. All the messages of God to man have related to this way of return and have been filled with the most urgent calls to come back by it and the most solemn warnings against refusing the voice of Him who speaks from heaven. And man needs a message of love from God for his conscience testifies against him and tells him of his sin and of God's just displeasure at sin and thus forbids the spirit of confidence while it commands the spirit of dependence. To such a one the gospel is indeed a welcome message for it tells him of the love of God to sinners and of His having provided an atonement for sin and of His open arms ready to embrace all who come to Him through this atonement, and thus the knowledge of the grace of God through Jesus Christ converts his dependence of necessity into a dependence of love and grafts him into the true vine.

Love Includes Pardon

Thou shalt love the Lord thy God with all thy heart, and mind, and soul, and strength, and thy neighbor as thyself. On these two commandments hang all the law and the prophets and the gospel.[16] They describe the perfection of man's spiritual state. They describe his confiding devoted dependence on the great root of the spiritual family and his fraternal sympathy with all the branches. When the love of the Creator is the dominant principle in the creature's heart, it keeps all the other principles and faculties and relations of the soul in their proper place. It is the true keystone of the arch that gives strength by maintaining order. It is the principle that connects the creature with the spiritual system and that receives of the fullness of the Creator. The fall of this keystone from its place in man's heart was and is the fall of man from his place in the family of God. Self and the creature took the place, and each man became an independent individual—loving and desiring and approving things according as they affected himself without regard to the will of God or the sympathies of the universal family. This is the fall and the sin and the misery of man—that the first and paramount relation does not have the first and paramount place in his heart—and that self—the principle of individuality—has usurped that place and has thus cut off the blessed

16. Matt 22:37–40.

communication between God and man that had been and could only be maintained through the channel of a supreme affection. And as this is the fall of man, so the restoration of man can be nothing other than the restoration of the love of God in the heart as the paramount principle in it and the due subordination of self and the creature under it. Any remedy that falls below this restoration falls below man's need. No pardon that leaves this undone is of any value to him. He needs no infliction from without to make him miserable, and it is not the removal of any outward infliction that can give him happiness. He must love God supremely. He must know that God is better than happiness, and that sin is worse than sorrow. It is not the desire of happiness, but the love of God that is the true keystone of the arch. "He that will save his life shall lose it, and he that will lose his life for My sake shall find it."[17] But if he loses his life not for Christ's sake but with the hope of saving it, he is out of the order of the blessing.

The remedy that God has given to man is the gospel. Its object is to displace self and the creature from the heart, to restore the love of God to the supremacy that is its due, and thus to restore man to his place in the happy family of God. The value of the gospel consists in its being a true representation of the gracious character of God in relation to His rebellious creatures. Jesus Christ is the subject of the gospel for He is God in relation to sinners. The gospel tells us how full of love He is towards sinners in all His feelings and in all His actions. It tells us of a love beyond utterance and conception, of His humbling himself even to the death of the cross for them, of His suffering for them on earth, and of His reigning for them in heaven. It tells us that this is our God, the God who made us and with whom we have to do, that this is He from whom we have been turning away with fear or hatred or disgust or indifference, and who yet has all along been thus loving us and has been putting forth His love to us continually in every breath that we draw and in all the care and protection and support that we experience, and it tells us all this that we may be constrained to love Him supremely and to choose Him for our portion and to depend on Him with an absolute confidence, and thus to have our individual will subordinated to His will. Before Christ came into the world, God had promised that He should come for no sooner had man fallen than he received an intimation of God's purpose of restoring him. There is something very striking in the form in which this first intimation of the Deliverer was given, and it appears to me that much instruction as

---

17. Matt 16:25.

to the nature of the gospel may be obtained by examining the characteristic features of it.

This intimation, as appears from the record in the third chapter of Genesis, was not addressed to our first parents themselves but formed a part of the sentence pronounced in their hearing against the serpent who had deceived them. "I will put enmity between thee and the woman, and between thy seed, and her seed, it shall bruise thy head, and thou shalt bruise his heel."[18] The most prominent feature in this sentence is that the serpent's head was to be bruised by a descendant of the woman.

This intimated to the human pair that it was the purpose of God to raise up a champion of their race who should avenge their quarrel with the serpent and undo what he had done at the expense of a slight hurt to himself. Now, as the work of the serpent had been to draw them away from the love of God, so the undoing of that work was to draw them back to the love of God—as the serpent's work had been to introduce sin and its consequences into the world, so the undoing of that work was to destroy sin and its consequences. And as this restoring work was to be done by a champion of the woman's seed, it would give to the human pair an assurance that their interests would be well regarded.

This sentence was pronounced on the serpent before Adam and Eve received their own sentence. They had endeavored to hide themselves from the presence of God. They had feared the worst. But they were now compelled to stand before Him and answer for themselves. They must have felt the futility of any excuses and anticipated the execution of the penalty pronounced against disobedience. As they stood trembling before their judge, they heard the sentence pronounced against their deceiver in which his final defeat and the subversion of his plans by one of their own descendants were predicted. And, although this prediction was in the form of a threatening against their adversary rather than of a promise of good to themselves, yet they could not but feel that it did contain a strong consolation for them. How could the serpent's head be said to be crushed while they continued the victims of his plots? The more they considered it, the more it would appear to them a prediction of their restoration. And after hearing this prediction, they would listen with greater calmness to their own sentence, and they would receive the different sorrows pronounced on them supported by the hope of the coming restoration.

18. Gen 3:15.

It is evident that this prediction did more than merely open up to Adam and Eve a distant prospect of the future retrieval of their ruined state. They must have found their feelings towards God and their relation to Him much altered by it. They saw that God had not abandoned them, and that His thoughts towards them were thoughts of compassion even while He was pronouncing sentence upon them. They saw that, although they were to be sent forth from paradise into the wilderness of the world, and although they were to be taught the evil of sinning against God by a life of suffering, yet the mind of God was even then planning their return, and that His love was even then preparing the means of accomplishing it. Would they not feel relieved by this discovery? They had feared the wrath of God—they knew that they had deserved it—and their consciences spoke terror to them. But they found that He pitied them, and that although they were to suffer, yet His love watched over them. Would they not feel that that which they had chiefly feared as the sting of suffering, even the wrath of God, was taken away, and that the thought of His compassionate care of them might well sweeten that cup of sorrow that their own hands had mixed and their own works had earned? Would they not say, "Nay, let paradise go since our God speaks to us in peace?" Would they not read in the kindness that gave this consolation an assurance that God had forgiven them? They had before been hiding themselves amongst the trees of the garden from His face, but now His face would be to them a refuge and a protection and a sun and a shield. They would wish Him to remain always with them for thus the wilderness would become paradise. They knew that He was the only power in the universe, and they knew that He had compassion on them for they could not doubt but that the consoling promise that He had put into their hearts proceeded from compassion. In whatever way the promise might be accomplished, its chief value lay in this that it was a demonstration and a pledge of God's love. They had felt themselves to be banished from His family and to be no longer His children, but this compassion of God proved to them that He was still their Father even when He chastised them, and that they were still His children even under chastisement. And thus, the promise of the Savior did for our first parents in a measure that which the Savior Himself, when He came in the flesh, did for all who received the testimony concerning Him. "As many as received Him to them gave He the privilege of being the sons of God."[19] It gave them the feelings

---

19. John 1:12.

and the privileges of children. It changed their dependence of necessity into a dependence of delighted choice. It taught them what to pray for and how to pray, for they knew that it was their Father's good pleasure and purpose that sin and sorrow and death should one day be abolished, and, therefore, they would pray for the coming of that day and for the advancement of the means necessary to its coming. And they would pray with confidence knowing their Father's love and knowing that their petition was according to his will.

I think that I have not attributed to this first intimation of the Savior any effect on the minds and feelings of Adam and Eve beyond what is conceivable and probable in their circumstances. And now I shall endeavor to explain the use that I wish to make of this case. I have supposed that Adam and Eve would immediately infer from the promise of the seed that God pitied them and had a gracious purpose of restoring them. And I have also supposed that this judgment which they formed of the compassionate feelings of God towards them would necessarily inspire them with confidence towards Him and would make them regard Him as a father who had forgiven them in His heart though He still protracted their suffering. And yet, there was not a single word spoken by God on that occasion directly pronouncing a present pardon or promising a future pardon. And therefore, their sense of pardon could only arise from a conviction that the promise of the Deliverer was a proof of a love towards them that necessarily included forgiveness in it. The belief of the existence of a benevolent feeling towards them in the mind of God could not but inspire them with some degree of confidence in Him, and when they knew that this benevolent feeling was actually occupied with a plan for undoing the evil that their fall had introduced, that confidence would rise nearer to assurance. Love seems to include pardon necessarily, and therefore the proof of the existence of love infers pardon as a necessary consequence. If they had not heard this intimation of a deliverance or if they had heard it without understanding that it was a promise of good to them, they would have had none of these feelings of confidence, and instead of exercising the privileges of the sons of God in speaking to their father and leaning on his omnipotent love, they would have shunned His presence and feared Him as their enemy. And yet the mind of God and the purposes of God towards them would have been precisely such as they now apprehended them to be—that is to say, their forgiveness in the heart of God would have been as much a matter of fact as they now saw it to be. The difference between their receiving the testimony and their not receiving it, therefore, was a difference affecting their own minds. It did not change the truth of the matter testified.

Hitherto God had never spoken to man on the necessity of faith in His testimony. He had never held out any promise to faith, and there was no apparent need that He should do so, for if the testimony were believed, it would necessarily do its own work, and if it was not believed, the work as necessarily remained undone. Faith, according to its degree, did for Adam and Eve all that it ever did or could do. The knowledge of the holy love of God entered their hearts by faith. They saw, though perhaps dimly, that it was the holy purpose of God to destroy sin, and yet that it was His gracious purpose to save the sinner. And they had peace through this conviction, that is to say, they were justified by faith. And here I will ask the reader if he thinks it possible that God gave them any premium on account of their believing the intimation? or that he pardoned them because they believed it? Surely not, or that He pardoned them in believing it as it is sometimes expressed, that is to say, that He bestowed on them belief and pardon at the same time? Doubtless all good things come from Him, but certainly this does not seem to me to be the true idea. The expression, "they were justified by faith," when applied to them would seem to me to signify simply this—that believing the reality of the love of God as expressed in the benevolent purpose that He had intimated to them respecting the future Deliverer, they took their forgiveness as included in it and looked with confidence towards God. This, I believe was their justification if they were indeed justified, and this I believe to have been the justification of every child of God from that hour to this, for I do not feel persuaded that any man ever receives or received anything in consequence of his belief of a truth other than the natural effect of that truth upon his mind.

If Pardoned, Why Punishment?

It will appear to many a strange sort of pardon that allowed the punishment to remain, for paradise remained barred, and the sentence of sorrow and of death remained unreversed. But God had spoken in their hearing of his gracious purposes respecting them, and that was forgiveness—the forgiveness that they needed—the forgiveness of their Father's heart though His hand might still, for a season, be heavy on them. And when we recollect the object of the gospel and the evil that it was intended to remedy, we shall feel that this was precisely the sort of forgiveness that was required. The hearts of the offenders were to be drawn back to the love of God for His own sake and not for His gifts. And it was part of the purpose of God to teach them to seek satisfaction in Himself by stripping them of His gifts and by making them feel their own insufficiency and thus leading them back to a childlike dependence on Himself. For it was not the penalty of the sentence that had cut them off from God's family. It was their own spirit of independence. It was that which had extinguished in them the principle of spiritual life and had cast them down from heaven by shutting God out from their hearts. And, therefore, a pardon that did not restore the spirit of dependence would still have left them miserable outcasts.

They had fallen by following their own selfish individual will rather than the universal will of the great Father of the spiritual family. And now God made them feel the bitterness of their own will and of their own root. He surrounded them with darkness and hopelessness, and then He presented to them His own holy will as the only light in the midst of the darkness and as the only refuge in the midst of the hopelessness, and thus He invited their dependence and urged them to return, and He taught them even by the terms of the promise to regard his holy abhorrence of sin as the only foundation of their hope. For the promise was that the serpent's head should be bruised, that is to say, that sin, self-will, and independence, as well as their consequences, should be rooted out. As long, therefore, as these evil principles continued to be the chosen counsellors of their hearts, such a promise could give them no comfort. But when they learned to look on sin as the enemy that had ruined them, then they would regard with delight God's avowed determination to exterminate it, and thus the holiness of God and His abhorrence of evil would be to them the pledges of their future deliverance. It is not the least important or striking feature in this first intimation of the gospel that it is thus expressed rather in the form of a threatening against sin than of kindness to the sinner. This was to show that there was no real kindness to the sinner that had not the effect of destroying sin, that the love of God was essentially a consuming fire to sin,[20] and that in the dealings of God with

20. Thomas Erskine's influence on later Scottish theologians is well known, but perhaps no more in evidence than by the direct connection between Erskine's thought here and George MacDonald's sermon "The Consuming Fire" in *Unspoken Sermons, Series I.*

regard to man, the restoration of happiness was less thought of than the restoration of holiness.

No pardon could be worthy of God or could possibly proceed from God that did not agree with and strengthen the sanctions of holiness. But this is not all. There can be no peace for a moral being that does not rest on the foundations of moral truth. If Adam had felt his own moral feelings compromised by his pardon, that pardon could never have given him peace—it could not even have given him the feeling of personal security—there would have remained a restless misgiving in his soul that all was not well for that the God of holiness must hate sin. There could be no way of giving true peace to the sinner except by making God's abhorrence of sin the very ground of the sinner's hope.

For the agony of Adam's mind could not have arisen merely from the fear of consequences. His conscience must have witnessed against him that through his offence, right and truth and holiness had been trampled on in the face of the universe and must have told him that until they were redressed, there was a stain on the moral government of God. But now from the sentence on the serpent, he understood that evil was to be destroyed, and right was to triumph. He saw that whatever might be the nature of God's purposes, the palliation[21] of the guilt of sin did not enter into them as the head of the rebellion was to be crushed. He thus felt assured that God made no compromise of justice when he spoke hope to the sinner.

The serpent's promised pardon was a mere impunity[22] in sin—"Ye shall not surely die," its object was to encourage sin. God's pardon embraced the destruction of sin, and its chief object was to restore to holiness. We have need to beware of mistaking the serpent's hiss for the grace of God. The hope of impunity given by the serpent encouraged Adam to yield to the promptings of his earthly desires. And the holy forgiveness of God encouraged and allured him to return back to God, not so much as a refuge from punishment for that seemed fixed—the wrath was past, and the suffering remained—but as a refuge from sin and from weakness and from earthly desires and from the assaults of that spiritual enemy who had stolen his jewel from him. And although the word of God is sparing of information with regard to the effect of the promise upon him, yet it is not inconsistent with the tenor of that information to hope and believe

21. Used in the sense of not excusing the sin or making it seem less serious.

22. Exemption from punishment.

that he who was the first offender was also the first monument of saving grace, and that with the promise, he received the spirit of the promise and the consolation of the promise into his soul. For surely never since has there been a created being that has stood in such need of a strong consolation. He had breathed the air of Eden and had been cast out of it—who has ever made such a shipwreck? He felt himself to be the author of a foul stain on the universe of God. He felt that his act was irretrievable, that he had opened a floodgate that he could not again shut and through which a dark tide rolled in overwhelming all the destinies that had been committed to his keeping. He saw this tide rolling in—he felt that it was his work, and he could not stop it. Verily he had need of a strong consolation. Whoever but he had his conscience burdened with the ruin of a world—the murder of an innumerable race of his own children. He knew somewhat of the value of the light of God's countenance—and he knew somewhat of the horror of its loss—he had tasted the good and the evil— and he felt that *his* heart and *his* hand had done the deed that had severed unborn numbers past numbering from the tree of life and had banished them from pleasant paradise, their destined place, and had made them outcasts from God and wanderers through a homeless wilderness. And whereas he had been entrusted by God for their [benefit][23] with the pearl of eternal life, he had cast it from him and instead of it had bequeathed to them the bitter cup of sorrow and death and a proneness to every crime and an exposure to every misery. What a blow must Cain's murder have given to his heart, and what a fearful sense must it have given him of the living and growing and spreading reality of that curse that he himself had brought upon his offspring, and as his prophetic spirit went down that troubled stream of human life that was to issue from him, would not each drop lift up in the ear of his conscience an accusing voice against him—and as the various forms of outrage and calamity succeeded each other, would his heart not wither with the thought "this is my work?"

But the gospel was sent to comfort all that mourn—and surely it comforted this father of mourners. It revealed to him the love of God. "This was the rest wherein his wearied spirit found rest, and this was the refreshing."[24] This love was the love of Him who was and is and shall be—the infinite in power and wisdom of Him who can make darkness light and crooked things straight, and He had pledged His faithful word

23. Original text has "behoof."
24. An allusion to Isa 28:12.

that He would undo this evil that had entered into the world. Adam had ruined his race and dishonored his God—earth had no portion, no comfort for him—but he looked forward to the day of the Deliverer, and he rejoiced to think that on that day God was to be glorified, and man restored.

When once he had learned this, he was in possession of the secret of the Lord—the secret of peace—for he would see the God of love in everything. He would see in every event a preparation for the coming of the Deliverer. In every affliction, he would recognize the plan of restoration. He would feel how well his present sorrows suited with his spiritual needs. He had fallen by seeking good, not in God, but in the creature. God's gifts had hidden God from his soul instead of being used as channels of communion with Him. And he was now stripped of these gifts, but he was stripped of them that he might learn that the Giver was better than the gift, and that as it was God who gave to Eden the whole of its charm, so even on the outside of Eden and in the absence of all gifts, God was Himself an overflowing fullness satiating every weary soul and replenishing every sorrowful soul. God's best gifts are no portion for man. He is Himself the portion of the soul—and so long as He is sought only for His gifts, He is himself unknown and un-prized.

The Restoration of All Things

There is another feature in this first intimation of the gospel that merits consideration—and that is its generality. It strikes at the selfishness and narrow individuality of will that had taken possession of that place in man's heart that ought to be filled by the wide will of God and by sympathy with the whole spiritual family. Its consolation is not a selfish consolation. It calls man to share in higher and more extended interests than his own personal safety. It makes personal safety a mere inference from the vindication of God's honor and the restoration of the race. This strikes me very much. We are led to infer our own pardon and interest in God's favor, not from any special declaration to ourselves, but from a manifestation of the holy love of God directed against sin and on behalf of sinners.

When I consider this important feature of the first promise, I cannot help thinking that the modern commentators on prophecy have reason when they say that the expectation of the restitution of all things occupies a much less space in the common announcements of the gospel or in the thoughts of Christians than it ought to do.[25] It is the chief feature of that gospel that was preached to Adam, and it is bequeathed to the church in the last words of inspiration as an enduring consolation and expectation—"behold I come quickly."[26] The general statements of the gospel in our days relate too exclusively to what is already past and to the individual salvation of each believer. Of course, it is impossible altogether to separate the doctrine of Christ's sacrifice from its general and future results, but these results seem to me not brought forward by preachers as they are in the Bible. I do not speak of the detail of these results nor of the particular fulfilment of the prophecies that relate to the last times because I do not feel myself qualified to speak on these subjects, but I speak of a fixed and longing expectation of the sure and fast approaching accomplishment of those promises that announce the final triumph of the Messiah, the establishment of His reign upon earth, the manifestation of the sons of God, and the full development of all those high privileges that arise out of their union with their divine Head.[27] This doctrine appears to me now in a very different light from what it once did. If the selfishness of individuality be really one of the chief elements in the fall of man, it might be expected that the divinely bestowed medicine for sick souls should contain an ingredient specially fitted to counteract and remove it. And such an ingredient I find in the universality of the declaration and purpose of the gospel that must necessarily impress its own character on the hope of everyone who rests upon it—for the first hope that any man can arrive at with regard to his own personal acceptance with God must be drawn from the great general manifestation of divine love directed to

25. Erskine is referring to Acts 3 and Peter's address to the Jews on the Temple Mount following the resurrection of Jesus. This is one of the earliest examples of how the gospel was preached by the apostles. Peter called for all hearing his voice to repent and be converted so that their sins may be blotted out when the "times of refreshing shall come from the presence of the Lord; and he shall send Jesus Christ . . . whom heaven must receive until the times of *restoration of all things.*" Included in the gospel was a word of consolation and the expectation that one day all of creation would be restored to harmony with God.

26. Revelation 22:20. The point being, with Christ will come "the times of restitution of all things" and the completion of God's declared plan to one day unite all things in heaven and earth in Christ (Eph 1:10, ESV).

27. Erskine assumes his readers are familiar with the prophesies of the *telos* or culmination of all things found in 1 Cor 15:20–28, Rev 5:9–10; 11:15, and Rom 8:18–25.

the destruction of evil and the restoration of the ruined race.[28] The individual drops are thus merged in the ocean, and self is lost in the "liberty, the universality, the impartiality of heaven."[29]

What Adam was thus taught to expect we yet look forward to. The champion has appeared, but evil is still spread over the earth, and the serpent's crested and uncrushed head still towers above it. But doubtless the work is going on that will accomplish the great prediction on which the destiny of our race hangs. We know that the government of the world is in the hand of God—and, therefore, we may rest assured that there is not a single link in the apparently perplexed chain of human things that does not connect with and guide to the coming glory—we may rest assured not only that all the histories of the kingdoms of this world are under the influence of an unfelt but irresistible control preparing the way for that kingdom that never can be moved, but also that personal events as well as national, private as well as public, are all under the same mandate, commissioned to lead on to the same great consummation.[30] This truth gives a seriousness and a dignity to everything. It banishes littleness from life because it connects all with the glory of God and the eradication of evil, and it seems to conduct us under the shadow of everlasting and omnipotent love where we may rest in peace until all calamities be [over and past].[31]

When the eye of the spirit is thus opened to see God working in everything and by everything to bring on the reign of righteousness, the heart will feel itself invited to the blessed privilege of entering into the purposes of God, of sympathizing with the everlasting counsels of His grace, of rejoicing in their assured success and of being a fellow worker with Him in every action of life. These actions may appear small and

28. Possibly a reference to Phil 2:10–11, "that at the name of Jesus every knee should bend, in heaven and on earth and under the earth, and every tongue should confess that Jesus Christ is Lord, to the glory of God the Father." It should be noted that the Greek word translated "confess" is *exomologeō* which means "to profess openly and joyfully."

29. Erskine is quoting from *The Spirit of Prayer* by William Law. Law (1686–1761) was an Anglican priest who is best remembered for his devotional work, *A Serious Call to the Devout and Holy Life*, a work that greatly influenced John and Charles Wesley, George Whitefield and others in the great Evangelical revival movement of the 1700s.

30. Erskine is referring to the great consummation or *telos* mentioned in 1 Cor 15:20–28 at which time Jesus Christ will reign triumphant, all evil will be eradicated, and God will be "all in all."

31. Replaced the archaic word "overpast."

insignificant in the world's judgment, but the believer knows that it is not in vain that the Ruler of the universe has called him to do all things to the glory of God. These are animating thoughts for poor wanderers in the wilderness who have listened to the Savior's voice. For them, the fall with all its sin and misery and darkness will soon pass away having served under the control of him who bringeth good out of evil to glorify the divine attributes and to introduce a high and holy and happy order of things—higher and holier and happier than that which Adam lost because founded on a nearer relation with God and a fuller manifestation of his character. The gate of Eden will once again be unbarred, and the banished ones brought back, and, in the meantime, though their path lie through the desert, yet that path is the way of holiness, and in it He will be with them whose presence can make the wilderness to be glad and the desert to rejoice and blossom like the rose.[32]

"Who Hath Redeemed Me and All Mankind"

I have remarked that if Adam actually had a sense of his personal acceptance with God, it must have been an inference that his heart naturally drew from the manifestation that had been made in this first promise of God's compassion for the offenders and of His purpose to destroy the evil that the serpent had introduced. And now I would say that I am persuaded that every descendant of Adam who has really understood that manifestation in any of its gradual developments, and especially in its last full development in the death and resurrection of Christ, must have had the same sense of his own personal acceptance with God. For only consider—the gospel reveals to us the existence of a fund of divine love containing in it a propitiation for all sin and a promise to destroy all the works of the devil—the sin—the misery—the death that he has introduced—and this fund is *general* to the whole race—every individual has a property [*possession*] in it of the same kind that he has in the common air and light of this world that he appropriates and uses simply by opening his mouth or his eyes. Is it not clear that as soon as any one really knows that such a fund exists, and that it is indeed the gift of God to the world and the common property of all the individuals in the world just as the natural air or light is, he will immediately infer his own particular interest in it and enter into the enjoyment of it, and he will make that blessed

---

32. Quoting Isa 35:1.

discovery that no tongue can rightly describe and no mere intelligence can rightly conceive even that he himself has a possession, an unalienable, an everlasting possession in the heart of God.

If I had offended a friend, and if I found that even before I had made up my mind to ask his forgiveness, he had risked his life for my sake, I might go immediately to confess my fault, but assuredly I should ask his pardon rather as acknowledging my offence than as expressing any doubt of his having already forgiven me. The risk of his life proved the gift of his love, and I should conclude that the greater gift of love included necessarily the lesser gift of forgiveness, and I should feel that I was doing wrong to that love if I even harbored a suspicion that he had an unforgiving thought of me. And this is precisely God's argument against the fears and suspicions of man. God commends His love to us in that while we were enemies, He gave His Son for us. Is not this just to meet the very need of our hearts? What more could be even imagined? And He gave His Son to the world, not only as a pledge of His love and an exposition of the nature of His love, but also as a treasury in which all things are actually contained that man can need or God bestow. When the vine gives itself to the branch, of course, the support and the sap of the vine are included in the gift. And as the giving of the vine to the branch includes all that the vine has to give, so the giving of Emanuel to the world includes all that God has to give. When we know this, we are justified by faith—that is to say, we assume our God's forgiveness as included in the gift of Himself. He neither loves nor pardons us on account of our belief in His testimony for it was while we were yet enemies and unbelievers that Christ died for us, but the belief of His love and of the gift that His love has bestowed will give a confidence that we are dearly welcome to Him—that we are His accepted ones—his adopted children. And while we do not know this or remain insensible to it, we are not justified—that is, we do not and cannot look to the holy God without distrust or terror—we have nothing but His condemnation for condemnation consists in the absence of His pardoning love, and that love is allowed to lie at our unopened door.

I know that justification is generally considered to mean pardon, or the imputation of Christ's righteousness, and I believe that very frequently it has this meaning in the Bible. But yet, I am persuaded by reasons that I shall afterwards explain that it also bears the meaning that I am now attributing to it, namely *a sense of pardon, or of the imputation of Christ's righteousness, or having the conscience purged of guilt,* and that *justification by faith* is a sense of pardon arising from a belief of that accepted propitiation that has been made for the sins of the whole world.

The terms in which the gospel has all along been proclaimed from the first sketch given to Adam down to the publication of it by the angels to the shepherds of Bethlehem and afterwards by our Lord Himself and His inspired messengers to the Jewish nation and to the world at large, seem to me to involve necessarily a universal and unconditional forgiveness of sin that is to stand in force during the period of man's life on earth, which on that account is called the acceptable time and the day of salvation— that is to say, they reveal God as the God of holy compassion—as the God who forgives iniquity, transgression, and sin through a propitiation made for the sins of the whole world—as the God who has anointed His only begotten Son to destroy the works of the devil and to introduce a new life as the God who says to all the ends of the earth, "Look unto Me, and be ye saved."[33] The reader may consult the following scriptures: Exodus 34:6, 7; Psalm 103:3, 10; Psalm 130:4; Isaiah 45:22; Isaiah 55:5; Jeremiah 9:23, 24; Luke 2:9–14; Acts 13:38; Romans 5:6, 8; 1 Timothy 1:15; 2 Corinthians 5:19; 1 John 2:2. In short, I am led to regard the pardon of the gospel as another name for holy compassion, that divine attribute for the manifestation of which I believe this world was created and thus as a part of the unchangeable character of God rather than as a particular act. It is a small thing to consider this pardon as a mere separate act removing penalties. And as it is a contracted [i.e., diminished] view, so also it is a false view for in fact it removes no penalties. Sorrow and death remain. The pardon of the gospel is not an *impunity*.[34] Nothing in truth is more opposite to its nature. It is the spiritual medicine for the eradication of sin from the heart. It is the seed of the woman who is to bruise the serpent's head. And thus, far from being a palliative[35] of sin, it is the condemnation of sin and the assurance of its destruction. For it is contained in that holy love of Christ that was manifested in his sacrifice to be a consuming fire to sin. It is a part of that holy love, and a part that cannot be disjoined from the whole. Christ is Himself the unspeakable gift of God to the world, and in Him all other gifts are contained. He is the gift that is laid down at each door—He is the sin-offering of which God spoke when He said to Cain,

33. Isa 45:22.

34. Exemption from punishment.

35. A medicine relieving pain without dealing with the cause of the condition.

"If you do not well, a sin-offering lies at the door"[36]—He is the new life not subject to death, and therefore, if we would have pardon and eternal life, we must have Christ for these gifts are in reality not separable from Him. They are modifications of Him—they are the ways in which He meets and supplies the wants of the sinner. If we receive not Him, we receive not them.

The pardon of the gospel is the form and body in which God reveals Himself to the sinner, and by which He invites the sinner's heart to receive Himself. It is "God in Christ reconciling the world to Himself, not imputing unto them their trespasses."[37] This is the pardon given to the whole world, and the belief of it pacifies the conscience of the believer and enables him to draw near to the true God with confidence, that is, the belief of this representation that God has given of Himself justifies the soul that believes in it. The pardon is the general manifestation of God to the world. Justification is the belief of that manifestation, and this is the true entrance into the church of Christ. God wills not the death of a sinner and has provided an atonement for sin, but those only who believe in it are saved by it.

The reader may perhaps wonder at my anxiety to establish a distinction between pardon and justification, a distinction he may think of absolute insignificance, but I think that it will appear to him of some considerable importance after weighing the following reasons. If pardon and justification be the same thing, or similar things, then we may substitute the one for the other, and as the Scriptures are quite clear on the point that sinners are justified by faith, it must be also true that they are pardoned by faith. Now what meaning is to be attached to this expression *pardoned by faith*. I can only conceive two meanings—the one is pardoned *on account* of faith, i.e. actually receiving forgiveness as a mark of God's approbation of faith; the other is taking pardon for granted or believing that we are pardoned. In the first of these meanings, pardon is really forgiveness. In the second, it is a *sense of forgiveness*, which is exactly what I understand by the term justification. In the first meaning,

36. Erskine is allegorizing Gen 4:7. This method of interpreting Old Testament scriptures in light of Christ and Him crucified was very common in the early church. While allegorical interpretation has its critics today, proponents are quick to point out that if Gal 4 and 1 Cor 10 are any indication, the apostle Paul was quite at home with this way of reading the Old Testament scriptures with an eye to their fulfillment in Jesus Christ. See Luke 24:44–47.

37. 2 Cor 5:19.

pardon is consequent on the faith and earned by it. In the second, the pardon exists before the faith and only becomes a matter of personal feeling in consequence of being believed. In the first case, there is a change on the sentence of the judge produced by the faith of the criminal. In the second, there is a change produced by it only on the feeling of the criminal himself.

Now if a man really looks to his faith in anything as the ground of his pardon or hope before God, he may be as much nourishing the spirit of independence and as much walking in that spirit as if he trusted in his obedience. Self is in the one case as well as in the other the axis on which the man turns and the root out of which he grows. And he can scarcely avoid falling into this error in some measure if he thinks there is no pardon for him until he believes. For if the pardon does not exist until he believes and immediately exists when he believes, surely his belief has something to do in making it. It is in vain to tell him that faith does not make it, but only receives it. For he may ask, where is it then before faith receives it? If my faith only receives it, it must have been in existence before my faith. The only idea that I can attach to the expression "receiving the pardon by faith" is that of believing in the pardon, but in order to this, the pardon must have been a real pardon before. If the gospel as it stands in the Bible actually includes my pardon, then it is clear that when I believe the gospel, I shall also believe my pardon as a part of it, and thus my faith will receive the pardon. But if the gospel does not in itself contain my pardon, how can my belief of the gospel be a receiving of pardon? The declaration of the gospel is that the Son of God "is a propitiation for the sins of the whole world,"[38] and that "through Him is preached unto men the remission of sins."[39] When I believe this, I must infer that He is a propitiation for my sins, and that remission of sins is proclaimed through Him to me because I am one of the whole world. It is also written that "God so loved the world as to give His only begotten Son, that whosoever believeth in Him might not perish but have everlasting life."[40] Now it is evident from the first clause of this sentence that the love of God does not flow from the sacrifice of Christ but is the source from which it flowed, and it is also clear that this love to the world is prior to and independent of their belief of it or of any of its effects. I am entitled, therefore, to take

38. 1 John 2:2.

39. Luke 24:47.

40. John 3:16.

this love to myself as being one of the world, and I must take the second clause of the sentence, not as any restriction or limitation of this love, which according to the record is as wide as the world but only as a solemn warning of the great guilt and danger that are incurred by allowing this love of God to lie on the outside of my heart and not receiving it into my heart as its best treasure even as the well of water springing up unto everlasting life.[41] According to this view, no one can possibly suppose that the love of God or the pardon of sin are the rewards of his faith or regard them in any other light than free gifts, which he may either receive or reject on his own responsibility. The love and the pardon are there whether he admits them or not. His faith merely receives them.

When the account reached me that the friend whom I had offended had risked his life for me, I read his forgiveness in this act of his love. I considered his forgiveness to be included in it, and therefore, when I believed it, or in other words, when my faith received it, my faith at the same time received pardon as a part of it. But if the account had been that my friend had risked his life for some other person, such a fact argued no love for me, and therefore I could not infer my own forgiveness from it, and thus, though I believed it, my faith would receive no pardon in it. My pardon was not contained in the act, and therefore, my belief of the act could give me no sense of pardon.

In like manner, if the gospel were that God only loved those who should believe in Christ, and that Christ died only for those who should believe in his sacrifice, it is clear that such a gospel does not embrace my pardon nor the assurance of God's love to me unless I am a believer, and therefore that my belief in such a gospel can give me no comfort nor peace until I first ascertain that I believe in Christ. And thus, my belief in Christ is made something distinct from a belief in the gospel and is only a prerequisite condition in order to my drawing comfort from the gospel, and thus also, pardon and the love of God are made rewards of faith in Christ. But this is not the gospel of the Bible, nor the view of faith contained in the Bible as every attentive reader of that blessed book must know.

The reader who is much accustomed to the ordinary technical language of theology will perhaps start at the idea of a universal and unconditional pardon alike independent of faith and obedience as if it were a removing of the landmarks of the church of Christ and a preaching of false peace to a world dead in trespasses and sins. But there is no such

---

41. John 4:14.

danger as he imagines. For this pardon is neither happiness nor heaven. Happiness and heaven consist in holiness, and pardon is only so far profitable to us as it produces holiness. It is contained in the gift of Christ, and in Him it is laid down at the door of each heart, but it cannot enter separate from Him, and until it enters it does nothing. When it enters, it then becomes justification and gives man confidence before the holy God. The declaration of pardon through Christ belongs to the whole world, but those only who believe this declaration have peace with God through it—that is, they only are justified, they only belong to the church of Christ.

This view of the subject is really the same with that which is given by the Church of England in her catechism. In answer to the question, "What dost thou chiefly learn by these articles of thy belief?" it is said, "First, I learn to believe in God the Father who made me, and all the world,—secondly, in God the Son *who hath redeemed me and all mankind,*—thirdly, in God the Holy Ghost, who sanctifieth me, and all the elect people of God." I mean no more by a universal pardon than what is expressed here. The redemption is universal—the limitation lies in the reception or application of it.

It is also the same view in reality with that which is often preached under the title of *a free offer of pardon* for what is a free offer of pardon, but a pardon laid down at our door?

In the life of Luther written by Erasmus Middleton, which is prefixed to the commentary on the Epistle to the Galatians, it is mentioned that in the Augustine Monastery at Erfurt where Luther made his profession, he had many conferences with an old monk on the article of remission of sins. This article was explained by the old monk to Luther to signify "that it was the express commandment of God that every man should believe his sins to be forgiven him in Christ." Luther then perceived the meaning of St. Paul when he repeats, "We are justified by faith." This is precisely the doctrine that I have been stating for it makes justification to consist in a belief that the remission of our sins is contained in Christ's propitiation. Justification changes nothing with regard to pardon. It is only the belief of a pardon that existed before, but which until it enters the heart is useless.

A very common idea of the object of the gospel is that it is to show how men *may obtain pardon* whereas in truth its object is to show how *pardon for men has been obtained.* And it is to present this most important truth (as I cannot but consider it) to some who may not have thought of it before that I have published this book—and it is for this same reason that

I have chosen to depart from the common phraseology on the subject—because I have found the common phraseology liable to misinterpretation. Thus, I have observed that even the phrase *free offer of pardon* is so interpreted that the very existence of the pardon is made to depend on the acceptance of the offer. The benefit of the pardon does most assuredly depend on its being accepted, but the pardon itself is laid up in Christ Jesus and depends on nothing but the unchangeable character of God.

This view of the doctrine is also distinctly stated by Luther in a passage on the nature of justification that occurs in the argument prefixed to his commentary on the Epistle to the Galatians. It is as follows:—"This is perfect righteousness (or justification) to know and believe this only that Christ is gone to the Father and is not now seen—that he sitteth in heaven at the right hand of the Father, not as a judge, but made unto us of God, wisdom and righteousness, holiness and redemption—briefly that he is our high priest entreating for us and reigning over us and in us by grace." It is obvious that the belief of these facts necessarily includes the belief of pardon. When this belief fades from the mind, justification fades along with it—as Luther goes on to say, "If there be any fear or grief of conscience, it is a token that this righteousness (justification) is withdrawn, that grace is hidden, and that Christ is darkened and out of sight." Luther evidently thought that anyone who understood the work of Christ, understood his own pardon to be contained in it—and he also considered righteousness or justification to be a *confidence of acceptance* necessarily connected with and inseparable from a present sense of the value of Christ's propitiation. This same doctrine seems to me also to be contained in two articles of the confession of faith of the French Protestant Churches, which are remarkably perspicuous on the subject of justification by faith.

> Nous croyons que toute notre justice est fondée en la rémission de nos péchés, comme aussi c'est notre seule félicité, comme dit David. C'est pourquoi nous rejetons tous autres moyens de nous pouvoir justifier devant Dieu; et sans présumer de nulls vertus ni mérites, nous nous tenons simplement à l'obéissance de Jésus Christ, laquelle nous est allouée, taut pour couvrir toutes nos fautes que pour nous faire trouver grâce et faveur devant Dieu. Et de fait, nous croyons qu'en déclinant de ce fondement tant peu que ce soit, nous ne pourrions trouver ailleurs aucun repos, mais serions toujours agités d'inquiétudes: d'autant que jamais nous ne sommes paisibles avec Dieu, jusqu'à ce que nous soyons bien résolus d'être aimés en Jésus Christ, vu que nous sommes dignes d'être haïs en nous mêmes.

Nous croyons que nous sommes faits partcipans de cette justice par la seule foi, comme il est dit, qu'il a souffert pour nous acquérir le salut, afin que quiconque croira en lui ne périsse point. Et que cela se fait, d'autant que les promesses de vie qui nous sont données en lui, sont appropriées à notre usage, et en sentons l'effet quand nous les acceptons; ne doutant point qu'étant assurés par la bouche de Dieu, nous ne serons point frustrés. Ainsi, la justice que nous obtenons par la foi dépend des promesses gratuites par lesquelles Dieu nous déclare et testifie qu'il nous aime.[42]

I subjoined a literal translation for the sake of those who do not understand the language.

We believe that all our righteousness is founded in the remission of our sins as it also is all our blessedness, as says David.[43] We therefore reject all other means of justifying ourselves before God, and without presuming on any virtues or merits of our own, we hold simply by the obedience of Jesus Christ, which is imputed to us to the end that our sins may be covered, and that we may find mercy and favor before God. And we believe that when we decline from this foundation however little, we can nowhere else find repose but must be always agitated by apprehensions inasmuch as we never are at ease with God until we are well assured of being loved in Jesus Christ seeing that we are worthy of being hated in ourselves.

We believe that we are made partakers of Christ's righteousness (i.e. that we are justified) solely by the belief that He has suffered for our salvation to the end that whosoever believeth in Him should not perish. And we believe that this justification takes place in as far as the promises of life that are given to us in Him are appropriated to our use, and we feel the effect of them when we accept them, not doubting that being assured by the mouth of God we shall not be disappointed. Thus, that righteousness that we obtain by faith hangs on the gratuitous promises by which God declares and testifies to us that He loves us.

It is clearly supposed in both these articles that the love of God manifested in the gift of Jesus Christ as a propitiation for the sins of the world really embraces the forgiveness of the sins of every individual, and it is therefore supposed that everyone who believes this great truth finds

42. Confession de Foi de La Rochelle—The confession of faith of the reformed churches of France known as the confession of faith of La Rochelle (1559).

43. Ps 32:1—"Blessed is he whose transgression is forgiven, whose sin is covered."

in it an assurance of God's love and favor to himself personally. And it is also supposed that this assurance and justification are one and the same thing. Were some great convulsions of nature to destroy all the human race but a single individual, the Bible with all its contents would belong to that single individual. It is addressed to Adam's race, and he would be the sole representative of the race, but we all and each of us belong to and represent Adam's race as much as such an individual, and we have therefore the same right in the contents of the Bible that he could have.

I am persuaded that faith in the gospel is always and must be always an *appropriating faith*, and that there is no true faith in the gospel which is not an appropriating faith. When a man opens his eyes upon the sun, he necessarily appropriates his share of its light, and he cannot look upon the sun without making this appropriation. In like manner, no man can look upon the sun of righteousness, which is the love of God manifested *in the making and the accepting of a propitiation for the sins of the world,* without appropriating his own share of its blessed light. He that believes really in the love of God to the world cannot but believe in the love of God to himself. The general belief and the appropriating belief are not two beliefs but one—just as the general receiving the light of the sun and the particular receiving our own share are not two receivings but one. God tells me in his word that He "is in Christ reconciling the world unto Himself, and not imputing unto them their trespasses."[44] When this message comes to me, can I put any other interpretation on it than that God is reconciling me and not imputing my trespasses to me? I think that any person who understands the meaning of these words and believes them to be the true words of God must believe himself pardoned. I shall here transcribe a passage from a very interesting account of the conversion of a young man who died at St. Helena[45] as the most satisfactory comment on the doctrine that I have been endeavoring to explain. "His faith seemed to have no mixture of imperfection in it for he simply and sincerely took for granted all that God said in His word and was astonished to hear any of us express our want of assurance of faith or of a constant and abiding sense of our personal interest[46] in Christ. This to him was a mystery

---

44. 2 Cor 5:19.

45. The story is told in "St. Helena Memoirs: An Account of a Remarkable Revival of Religion that Took Place at St. Helena During the Last Years of the Exile of Napoleon Buonaparte" by Thomas Robson, published in 1827, a year before Erskine's book.

46. Not interest as in wanting to know or learn about Christ, but in the sense of having a rightful share in Christ, having a participation and advantage in Christ.

we never could explain, and which happily for himself, he died in entire ignorance of." Surely of such is the kingdom of heaven. Happy man!—he had opened his mouth and God had filled it. We need go no further than this to understand the nature of the assurance of faith. A present sense of the full value of the atonement and of the love of God revealed in it will always give assurance, and when that sense decays, the assurance must decay if it is not a mere fiction of the imagination.

Let no one think this point a mere curious and speculative question of abstract theology for it is in truth a question of real practical religion—*it is a question whether man will consent to be a receiver—a mere receiver—or not.* He is naturally unwilling to be a receiver for the fall of man consists in the spirit of independence—in the setting up of self in the place of God—in an averseness to be a receiver. Now can there be anything so subversive of the principle of independence in him—so humbling to self—and so well fitted to restore to him the character of a mere receiver—as the knowledge of the fact that he can positively do nothing towards his own deliverance, and that his only escape from absolute ruin, his only hope for time and for eternity lies in a free, unsolicited, unthought of, and most costly gift of love laid down at his door by that God whom he has been neglecting and despising and resisting from his youth up until now.

Why the Gospel Is an Offense to Man

It is a principle of common sense—as it is a principle always taken for granted in the Bible—that the ground of a man's hope and expectation and dependence must command his will and mold his character. As long as he depends on himself or has hope of delivering himself by his own exertions, so long will he hold and maintain the independence of his own will. He may wish to do many things that are right, and he may do many things that are honorable to himself and useful to others, and yet all the while it is not the will of God but his own will that he follows. Nothing short of an absolute despair of delivering himself or helping himself at all can cut the roots of his self-will. And nothing short of an absolute dependence on God's unmerited grace for everything can graft him on the root of God's will. And thus, nothing but a true sense of the absolute unconditional gratuitousness of the gospel can write the law of God on the heart of man. And yet this doctrine of gratuitousness is opposed as if it were antinomian. But the true reason of the opposition is that it opposes the pride of man. *He therefore opposes it.* There is indeed something very striking in the perverse ingenuity with which he endeavors to dilute the medicinal virtue of the gospel. He *must* have self to lean on, and so when he is obliged to surrender *his own works,* he [resorts to][47] *his own faith* as his prop. But this is still *self,* and in whatever form it appears, as long as it is the ground of hope, it must command the will. And surely this is the chief reason why the gospel contains so many evident declarations on the part of God that beside him there is no Savior,[48] and that man is absolutely incapable of doing anything in the work of his own redemption, and that his interference only spoils it. Anything of man's *own* must be bad—because the growing out of his own root is itself the original offence and disorder—he ought to be a branch and not a separate plant. I am quite satisfied that *self* is the great antinomian,[49] *because* it is the great antichrist—and that where *self* acts in this matter and tries to establish a claim to the benefits of Christ's death either by faith or by works, it incapacitates us for spiritual obedience by cutting us off from the true source of spiritual life.

Thus, we may in some measure understand how the very gratuitousness of the gospel may lead to its rejection, because this very gratuitousness is in fact a declaration on the part of God that man can do nothing for himself, and thus it is an offence to his pride. But it is not pride only, but everything that is unholy in the human heart that is offended by the gospel. For the deliverer revealed in it is the promised champion who is to destroy the works of the devil. Those, therefore, who cleave to evil cannot welcome the gospel for they cannot rejoice that evil is to be destroyed. Its destruction is their destruction, the destruction of their joy and occupation, and though they may desire impunity, they cannot embrace that as good news that tears their idol from them. Evil is the strong man armed who holds their hearts and wills and thoughts and desires, and they cannot bear to hear of that stronger than he who, under the form of a pardon, would take his armor from him and cast him out of his usurped hold in the heart. They take part with the strong man against the stronger, and they feel his defeat and ruin to be their own. And they will

---

47. *Archaic* "betakes himself to."

48. E.g., Isa 43:11; 45:21; 49:26; Hos 13:4.

49. Dictionary.com: "a person who maintains that Christians, by virtue of divine grace, are freed not only from biblical law and church-prescribed behavioral norms, but also from all moral law."

find it so—they will find themselves involved in his fate if they adhere to his party. And that fate is to be crushed.

In the meantime, however, the pardon stands at the door, and the deliverer is in it and knocks for admittance. The pardon is universal, and still it may with perfect propriety and consistency be said that until man receives it into his heart, he is under condemnation. For he is excluded or excludes himself from the only good and joy in the universe—he is away from the God of love, and thus he is full of wrath and encompassed with wrath—he is away from the God of light, and thus he is in outer darkness, and this is and must be his inheritance until he admits the gospel into his heart. It is quite evident, then, that a man may be thoroughly and forever miserable although he has this pardon, and that he can derive no possible benefit from it except by believing it.

But when a poor sinner comes to know that God is his true friend who has loved him and evil his true enemy that has ruined him—that God has a right to all his heart and to be the first and the last in all his ends and aims—and that evil is a usurper whose reign over him is a reign of injustice and darkness and hopelessness. Oh! this knowledge is the powerful persuasion of the Spirit within him, and he opens the door of his heart, and he welcomes in the pardon chiefly because with it and in it there comes that stronger than the strong man who will cast out the usurper and chase away his darkness and wrath and injustice and lies and bring in a reign of righteousness.

And he expects no reward for admitting the deliverer into his heart other than the delight of having this new and better reign within him. It is God's holy love that he believes, and it is the enjoyment of that holy love that he enters into by believing it and into that only.

When a man says, "I believe the gospel, and therefore I am warranted to expect pardon and eternal life," I cannot but have doubts whether he understands the gospel. For if he did understand it, I do not think that he would look further than the gospel itself as the reward of his faith. Let me suppose the case of a mother whose only child has been stolen from her in infancy and whose heart still bears the fresh and unclosed wound of her loss and whose imagination is continually haunted with dark and busy thoughts as to what the present condition and future fate of her child may be. I discover the child and find it all that a mother could wish or love. I come to her and say to her that I have news for her, and that she will be richly rewarded if she believes it. I then tell her my news. Oh, reader! do you think that she would ask me what reward I meant to give her for believing?

The good which we receive from believing in the love of God manifested in Christ Jesus is analogous to that which we receive from believing in the worth and kindness of a human friend—only that the one is as nothing in comparison with the other. It is nothing other than the enjoyment of God in Himself and in His creatures. It is not anything that we get on account of our loving Him, but it is the happiness of loving Him and knowing ourselves to be loved by Him. It is dwelling on and in His high perfections. It is giving Him our perfect sympathy and receiving His. It is knowing Him as the infinite God and yet as an affectionate Father, as a friend that sticks closer than a brother. It is the assurance that the heart draws from His love in giving His Son and perhaps from some more special and personal tokens of that love, that He will never leave us nor forsake us, that He will never cease to love us with a love that will be and must be our satisfying and filling and delighting portion through all eternity. It is the joyful and confident anticipation of the day when the mystery of God shall be accomplished and the glory of the Lord shall be revealed, and when the children of God shall he glad and rejoice forever in the new heavens and the new earth that their Father will create. It is the discovering that all the works of creation—all events—time and space—eternity and infinity—everything is full of that God who loved us and gave Himself for us, and who in giving us Himself freely gives us all things. This is the good that a soul gets by believing the gospel, and is it not enough or shall we still ask whether we are warranted to expect pardon and eternal life because we believe the gospel? Does not such a question indicate a radical mistake as to the meaning of the gospel? Is it not the question of a man who sees nothing in the gospel itself to satisfy him and therefore supposes that there must surely be something else to accompany it in order to make it that desirable thing that it is said to be? Is it not the question of a man who considers his belief of the gospel nothing other than a meritorious submission of his reason to the authority of God—a submission that is to be rewarded by some mark of his approbation?

Justification Not a Recompense for Believing

And now I ask the candid reader whether this expectation of receiving some reward for believing the gospel is not very like the common view of the doctrine of justification by faith? If justification be pardon or a judicial act of God imputing Christ's righteousness to a sinner—and if this act has no existence until he believes the gospel, then justification is not received by faith but bestowed on account of faith. It is a recompense for believing, and men are not blessed in the gospel itself but on account of their belief of it. Whereas if justification means a sense of pardon through a propitiation or, as it is called in the epistle to the Hebrews 9:9–14, *the being made perfect as pertaining to the conscience,* and *having the conscience purged from dead works,* then all is simple for we can have no difficulty in seeing that a sense of our own personal pardon and acceptance must arise out of a belief that a propitiation has been made by the holy love of God for the sins of the whole world. *This justification* is truly and intelligibly *by faith* for it necessarily and naturally results from a belief of the love of God revealed in the general atonement accomplished by the obedience of Jesus Christ unto death for the sins of the world. But if we do not understand the atonement of Christ—if we do not see in it such an expression of forgiving love and such a satisfaction to justice as may engage our confidence and purge our consciences—then our belief in the atonement can do us no good—it does not justify us. It does not comfort nor strengthen us. It is a well to us without water. And in this way, when no comfort is derived from the atonement itself, an endeavor is made to draw comfort from the *belief* of the atonement as an act to which God is supposed to have promised acceptance and a special blessing. I see no such promise in the Bible. There are exceeding precious promises to those who trust in God and wait on God, but the promise of pardon as the reward of faith in anything seems to me a mere human invention in direct opposition to the whole tenor of the gospel.

It is evident from Romans 5:1 that justification is necessarily connected with peace of conscience—"being justified by faith, we have peace with God"—but pardon unknown or unbelieved will not and cannot give peace of conscience. Justification, then, is not pardon simply, but pardon known and believed—pardon implied in and inferred from a gift greater than pardon. Romans 3:20, "By the deeds of the law shall no flesh be *justified,* for by the law is the *knowledge of sin."* The knowledge of sin or the sense of sin is placed in direct antithesis to justification, which therefore ought to mean a sense of pardon. The deeds of the law in this passage appear to me to mean the expiatory and purifying rites of the law. And when the Apostle says of them that no flesh shall be justified by them for by the law is the knowledge of sin, he means to express precisely the same idea that is more fully explained in the Epistle to the Hebrews, chapters 9 and 10, [that is to say]⁵⁰ that these rites were intended rather to keep up a sense of sin than to give a sense of pardon. They removed ceremonial pollution, but they could give *no peace to the conscience* except by referring the worshipper to that great sacrifice of which they were only shadows. The law, in its addresses to those who are under it, always supposes them to be sinners, i.e., *under condemnation*. It knows nothing and teaches nothing about *that new life* which is communicated by Christ to those who come to him and that *is not under condemnation*. The law supposes men always to be growing out of a root that is under the condemnation of death. The gospel reveals a fountain *of new life,* even the life of God in Christ Jesus that *cannot fall under condemnation* because it is the life of God—and this is the fountain to which all are invited. This same idea is expressed by Paul in the Epistle to the Galatians, chapter 2, where he gives his reasons for condemning Peter's conduct at Antioch. If I seek to quiet my conscience (he argues) by the rites of the law, do I not deny the sufficiency of Christ to atone for my guilt and to clear my conscience? "But if while we seek peace of conscience through Christ, we yet be found to have our consciences laden with a sense of condemnation, do we not falsely represent Christ as a dispenser of condemnation, instead of a dispenser of pardon, which he really is?" If the knowledge of Christ leaves my conscience still burdened by a sense of guilt, then either Christ is not the dispenser of the divine mercy or my knowledge of him is miserably defective. I refer chiefly to the 17th and 18th verses of the second chapter. "But if while we seek to be justified (to have our consciences purged of the sense of guilt) by Christ, we ourselves also are found sinners (still laboring under a sense of condemnation), is therefore Christ the minister of sin (the dispenser of condemnation)? Far be it. For if I build again the things which I destroyed (the necessity of the Jewish ceremonial which Peter had been going into), I make myself a transgressor." I also quote the passages from the Epistle to the Hebrews.

Hebrews 9:9. "Which was a figure for the time then present, in which were offered both gifts and sacrifices, that could not make him that did the service perfect as pertaining to the conscience." Verse 14. "How much more shall the blood of Christ, who, through the eternal Spirit offered Himself without spot to God, purge your consciences from dead works to serve the living God?" Chapter 10:2. "For then would they not have ceased to be offered? because that the worshippers once purged

50. Replaced viz.

should have had no more conscience of sins?" Verse 22. "Let us draw near with a pure heart, in full assurance of faith, having our hearts sprinkled from an evil conscience, and our bodies washed with pure water."

From these passages I am led to infer that the faith of the gospel attaches to and takes hold of the propitiatory sacrifice of Christ as including and implying in it the pardon of sin and thus delivers the conscience from the sense of unpardoned sin. And I am also led to infer that this deliverance from the sense of unpardoned sin by the knowledge that a propitiatory sacrifice has been made is just another expression for justification by faith because similar effects are ascribed to them both, [that is to say] "peace with God" and "boldness" and "full assurance" before Him. Man, in order to his well-being and right-being, must walk with God and must depend on Him, but he cannot and dare not do this while he feels the weight of unpardoned sin on his conscience. But when his soul hears the good news that a propitiation for sin has been made and accepted, he can look on God as his father and dares to depend on Him and to expect great things from Him. "He may then draw near with a true heart and full assurance of faith"[51] and ask and receive the blessing.

I know that all those who are really taught of God will feel themselves debtors to His mercy alone, whatever their theory may be. But even these persons, although their true feeling may save them from the full effect of their erroneous theories, may be much perplexed and hindered by them. But assuredly there are many who do really consider their faith as the fulfilment of a condition by which they are entitled to pardon and eternal life. They conceive pardon and eternal life to be rewards bestowed on those who believe as marks of God's approbation of faith. Of course, then, when they wish to confirm their assurance of their salvation, they will look to the accuracy or to the unquestioning submission of their faith—and they will endeavor to persuade themselves that seeing they believe accurately and unhesitatingly, surely God will give them eternal life. They will repeat, "Believe on the Lord Jesus, Christ, and thou shalt be saved"—and they will say we believe in the Lord Jesus Christ—therefore, we shall be saved. And if they find misgivings in their minds, they will endeavor to take comfort and encouragement from the reflection that as they have not doubted the Christian doctrines, so they must be within the pale of that covenant that promises all things to faith. I am confident that such reasonings as these never can give peace to a really awakened

---

51. Heb 10:22.

conscience. The moral feelings refuse such comfort. It cannot but appear strange to a moral and thinking being that God should pardon him because he believes something. It gives such an unintelligible and unedifying idea of the divine character—an idea that never can impress the mind with holy feelings or affections or desires. And then when the hour of weakness and apprehension comes—when I feel myself on the brink of the unseen eternity—am I then to draw my comfort from this dry cistern "that I have believed certain facts?"—and is it not likely that I may then anxiously inquire has my faith been of the right kind?—and I may think surely if it had been so, it would have had a more sanctifying influence on my conduct through life and would now impart to me a greater peace. I can conceive nothing in this world more melancholy than the situation of a man lying on his deathbed who has before his mind all the rich treasures of the gospel but does not see how he is to connect himself with them. He sees in the Bible the promises of God's everlasting love and of the gift of eternal life—but he does not see them as his own—and he asks what and where is the link that unites a sinner to these unutterable blessings? Oh, it is an inquiry full of agony when death is evidently not many hours distant! If he is told that faith is the link that unites the sinner to the promises, he looks into himself to see whether his faith is right—and he cannot tell whether it is or is not, and his perplexity rises above his strength or his endurance, and his agitation makes it impossible for him to know or examine what the state of his belief is. Would it not be a blessed message to that soul to tell him that Christ died not for believers but for the world, that He was promised as a deliverer before there was one penitent or believing thought in any human breast, and that when He did appear on earth, He said of Himself that He came "to seek and to save that which was lost,"[52] and His invitation was, "come unto Me all ye that are weary and heavy laden, and I will give you rest."[53] God revealed these joyful truths to men, not that they might be rewarded for believing them, but that they might have much peace in resting on them, and that their hearts might be filled with much love and gratitude in thinking of and feeding on the kindness of that God who has had mercy on them.

Would it not be good tidings of great joy to him to tell him that Christ had been given as a propitiation for the sins of the whole world, and "that in Him God was reconciling the world unto Himself, not

52. Luke 19:10.

53. Matt 11:28.

imputing unto them their trespasses"[54] that thus the full pardon was already given to him before he had thought of asking it, and that what now remained for him was to bless God for His unspeakable gift and to ask for that spirit that might open his understanding and his affections to appreciate and to feel the value and the love of the gift? When the poor man believed this, he would be justified by faith—he would have the sense of pardon and acceptance before God—and he would speak to Him as to a father who pities His own children. Before he believed this, he was one of that world that God so loved as to give His Son to be a propitiation for its sins, but while he remained ignorant of that love and unbelieving, he was not justified by it, his conscience remained unpurged—he neither knew his sin nor his pardon—he had no childlike confidence in God—he had no share in eternal life.

There is something very delightful and very satisfying in this way of drawing hope and encouragement for the future from past acts or expressions of love. And it is connected very intimately with the spirit of dependence. It is a style of thought and feeling that seems to me to run through all the Bible and to be its peculiar characteristic. I cannot refrain from giving some examples of it, although it may appear to some of my readers a departure from the direct line of the argument.

Examples to Consider

When our Lord asked water from the woman of Sychar at Jacob's well, she reminded Him of the dissensions between the Jews and the Samaritans as a reason that ought to have prevented Him from making such a request—He answered her, "If thou knewest the gift of God, and who it is that saith to thee give Me to drink, thou wouldst have asked of Him and He would have given thee living water."[55] Such is the love of man to man—the Jew refuses water to the Samaritan and the Samaritan to the Jew—but such is not the love of God. His love is a free and boundless love that gives to all men liberally and [does not utter reproaches.][56] If she had known the fullness of that love, how disposed to give, and how much it had already given unasked, and if she had known that He who now spoke to her was Himself the great gift of God to a lost world and the

54. 2 Cor 5:19.
55. John 4:10.
56. Archaic: "upbraideth not."

dispenser of all other gifts, she would have profited by this opportunity and instead of speaking of the quarrels of men, she would have asked for the blessing of God—she would have asked and He would have given her living water. A knowledge of God's love and of His past gift of love is the true source of confiding dependence and assured hope for the future. There is something unspeakably touching in that simple expression, "thou wouldst have asked, and He would have given thee." He seems to regard His giving as the natural consequence of her asking, and it is so for He has already given the gift, and the creature's asking is the mere opening of the heart to admit a love which has been long waiting at the door. And He gave her the living water. He had come there to give it to her. He had passed through Samaria on purpose that she might know the gift of God—and He did not leave her until she knew that the Spirit of God was a spirit of [giving],[57] and until she had asked and received the living water. What He said to her was to awaken in her a sense of need and a desire of supply and to make her acquainted with the great Giver and the great gift—her heart opened, and the blessing entered. As soon as she knew the love of God in the gift of the Savior to a sinful world, she was justified by faith, she took her pardon and acceptance as included in the gift, and she asked for the bread and the water of life without fear of a refusal. She asked and He gave. This argument for present confidence and future hope drawn from past kindness pervades the Old Testament as well as the New. I may mention one beautiful example of it in the 51st chapter of Isaiah. As the prophet is contemplating the fallen state of Israel, he thus draws encouragement from the former dealings of God in their behalf—

> Awake, awake, O arm of the Lord! Art thou not it which hath cut Rahab (Egypt) and wounded the dragon? Art thou not it which hath dried up the fountains of the great deep; and made a way through the sea for the ransomed to pass over? *Therefore,* the redeemed of the Lord *shall return,* and shall come with singing unto Zion; and everlasting joy shall be upon their heads; they shall obtain gladness and joy, and sorrow and mourning shall flee away.[58]

With what confidence does he draw his conclusion! He passes from the past deliverance to the future as if the one necessarily grew out of the other. This is an argument worth a thousand syllogisms for it speaks to

57. Replaced "givingness."

58. Isa 51:9–11.

the heart, and the only argument in religion that is worth anything is that which does speak to the heart. I cannot but transcribe the words that follow those that I have last quoted. They are words that some sorrowful heart may be glad to read for they are the words of Him who made the heart and sends it sorrow and can make sorrow a greater blessing to it than joy. "I, even I, am He that comforteth you."[59] Who need remain uncomforted when there is such a comforter? Oh! taste and see that the Lord is gracious. Blessed is the man that puts his trust in Him.[60] This is the manner of the Bible. It tells us of the streams that it may allure us to the fountain. It tells of the past acts of God's faithful love that we may be led to set our hope on God and to feel assured that He who has helped will help, and that He who has loved will love unto the end. "God hath so loved the world, as to give His only begotten Son for it";[61] "and will He not with Him freely give us all things?"[62] It is impossible to doubt it. That great gift includes all other gifts for it is God Himself. It is not a stream from the fountain but the fountain itself, the unsparing and inexhaustible fountain of eternal love. And it is given to the world. And therefore, as each and every Israelite might take to himself encouragement and consolation from the past interpositions of God on behalf of his nation, so each and every child of man may draw rich and abundant encouragement and consolation from this past act of God's holy love on behalf of the world. And it is indeed a full fountain. It contains all other gifts and is contained in them all—it is their very spirit and life—it gives them all their value and all their sweetness—and without it they are empty husks. But the selfish grossness of man's evil heart greedily seizes on these lower gifts while it rejects the love of God contained in them, which is their very soul. And thus, they become husks—the husks on which the poor prodigals of the world are feeding. The bread of our Father's house is the love of God in Christ Jesus, and there is enough of it and to spare—and we might find it even enclosed in these very husks if the mouth of our spirit were opened as the mouth of our sense is, if the desire of our heart were after God instead of being after self-gratification. Does it not seem strange that such a Father should have so many prodigals, and that the swine and the husks in this far country should be so much preferred to the society and

59. Isa 51:12.

60. Ps 34:8.

61. John 3:16.

62. Rom 8:32.

the bread of our Father's house? Yet it is not that the swine and the husks satisfy anyone. They are seen by many in their true loathsomeness and emptiness, but *self* can live amongst them—that is the secret—whereas a man must renounce self before he says in earnest, "I will arise and go to my father." This is the only bar which separates man from God for God's arms are open.

It appears to me further that the invitation to prayer is itself an act of forgiveness. And the invitation to prayer is universal. Whoever will make use of it may make use of it. There is no limit but in the will of man. The proof of this is contained in the denunciation of Peter of Simon [the sorcerer]. Acts 8:20–24 is very strong. He tells him that he is in the gall of bitterness and bond of iniquity, and yet he desires him to pray. And never has there been a prayer lost. Some of my readers may recollect an anecdote told of Buonaparte,[63] which in some degree illustrates my meaning. When the Duc d'Enghien[64] was apprehended, it is said that he begged much for a personal interview with Buonaparte. This, however, Buonaparte decidedly refused and being afterwards asked his reason for doing so, he replied, "I should have been obliged to pardon him if I had admitted him, and I had resolved that he should die." Hear what this unjust judge says—he would have considered the reluctantly granted admission of his victim into his presence as inferring a pardon—surely then he would have considered his own pressing invitation to him to come into his presence as still more strongly inferring a pardon. If that hard man felt thus, what shall we conclude from the invitations that the God of love makes to all? What shall we conclude from the invitations of him who does not will the death of the sinner, but that all should turn and live? of him who said, "Come unto Me all ye that are weary and heavy laden, and I will give you rest?"[65] It may be said that it is only the prayer of faith that is heard. This is true, but every prayer to God is a prayer of faith. It is not and cannot be a prayer at all without the belief that "God is, and that He is the rewarder of them that diligently seek Him."[66] We may pray for faith. We may pray for the spirit of prayer. We may pray for the

---

63. Napoleon Bonaparte, at the time, First Consul of France.

64. Or Duke d'Enghien, the title belonging to Louis-Antoine-Henri de Bourbon-Condé who was executed in 1804 by Napoleon Bonaparte for allegedly aiding the British and plotting against France. The charge was never proven, and the execution shocked the aristocracy of Europe as the duke was of royal lineage.

65. Matt 11:28.

66. Heb 11:6.

waiting eye and the hungering and thirsting after righteousness. We may pray for the first elements of Christian light and feeling just as well as for the communications of heavenly joy and the greatest advancements in the divine life. But the first breathing or cry of the heart after these things implies faith in God. And such prayers, if real, are prayers in the name of Christ because they are prayers for the accomplishment of that work that Christ came from heaven to do. The name of God is not the word *God* but the revealed character of God, and the name of Christ is the character of God revealed in Christ—the character of holy love consuming sin and saving the sinner. He came to destroy the works of the devil—this is His name—and a prayer against the works of the devil is a prayer in His name being according to the will and counsel of God revealed in Him. This seems to be the meaning of that frequently recurring expression, "in the name of Christ." When the heart goes along with the declared purpose of God to eradicate evil and bring in the reign of righteousness—it prays in the name of Christ—it lives and moves and has its being in the name of Christ. Prayer seems to suppose an open ear and a forgiving heart, and when God commands it, He seems to manifest Himself as the hearer of prayer and the forgiver of sins.

Addressing a Radical Error

It appears to me that this view of pardon as being a manifestation of the divine character in Christ Jesus altogether independent of man's belief or unbelief is a view much fitted to draw the soul from self to God and thus to sanctify it at the same time that it gives it peace, because it presents to it a ground of hope entirely out of itself that remains unchanged and unaffected by the fluctuating feelings of man's heart, and because that ground is the holy God. It is not a pardon distinct from God, but it is the holy God manifesting Himself in a pardon. This view also represents the holy love of God as the one fountain out of which all comfort and strength, all hope and all holiness, are to be drawn, and it represents this fountain as perfectly and absolutely open and accessible to all the children of men at all times. Whereas when a man thinks that he is not pardoned until he believes, he is almost necessarily drawn to *self* and to seek comfort in the [doings][67] of his own mind, and as he does not conceive himself entitled to draw water out of that fountain of holy love until he has satisfactorily

---

67. Replaced "actings."

answered to himself the question, "do I believe or not," so after he thinks that he has satisfactorily answered that question, he considers the water to be the reward of his belief. This is one reason, and I think a strong one for pressing the absolute freeness of pardon and the distinction between it and justification, and I shall now give another. While pardon is conceived to depend upon faith, and while it is confounded with eternal life, it is exceedingly difficult to press the warnings and precepts and exhortations of the Bible as the Bible itself presses them. If pardon and eternal life are by faith alone, what is the use of obedience? And how can the preacher urge it as absolutely necessary without some inconsistency in his plan of instruction? The usual way of escaping from the difficulty is to urge holy obedience as *an evidence* of the reality of faith as if the value of holy obedience consisted not in itself, not in its own conformity to the will of God, but in its being an evidence of the existence of faith in our minds. According to this system, a preacher might exhort his hearers "to love the Lord their God with all their hearts" upon the ground that if they did not, they would want an important evidence of the reality of their faith. Is this a worthy argument for urging men to the exercise of that high duty and high privilege on which hang all the law, all the prophets, all the gospel? And must not there be a radical error in that system that leads many a faithful servant of God to use such an argument? The *whole use of the gospel* is that the holy love of God may be introduced into man's heart and work there its own likeness. But the gospel cannot enter the heart without being believed, and here is the *whole use of faith.* The duty of the creature to love the Creator and the other creatures of that Creator for His sake ought to be pressed as the most positive obligation resulting from our relation to Him and His goodness to us—as constituting the height of moral and spiritual perfection—and as being the very substance out of which all true happiness is composed. The end of the commandment is love out of a pure heart and a good conscience and faith unfeigned.[68] It is more befitting that faith in the gospel should be pressed and prized as producing holy love in the heart and life than that holy love should be pressed as an evidence of faith.

There is a third reason that seems to me of great weight for giving this view of pardon. According to the common system, pardon is sought as an end and not as a means to an end. This gives a contracted and mercenary tone to the mind. Pardon is the bread from heaven rained round all our

---

68. 1 Tim 1:5.

habitations. It is the bread on which the soul must feed to strengthen itself for the daily work. As long as we look on pardon as the ultimate in religion and not as a thing already possessed, it is impossible that we can thus feed on it, and unless we feed on it, we neither can have peace nor strength. The pardon truly is Jesus Christ, and he has himself told us, "Except ye eat my flesh, and drink my blood, ye have no life in you."[69]

Consideration of Some Passages on Forgiveness

But are there not many passages in the Scriptures that seem decidedly to teach that forgiveness is not a general but a particular gift bestowed only on those who believe in Jesus Christ? We shall examine some of these passages, but before doing this, I would beg the reader to consider attentively the expressions contained in 2 Corinthians 5, verses 19, 20, and 21. God is there set forth as "in Christ, reconciling the world unto Himself, not imputing unto them their trespasses." I ought to observe that the word *reconcile* has a sense in the New Testament somewhat different from what is usually attached to it in ordinary language. The Bible never speaks of God *being reconciled* but only *as reconciling; to reconcile* is the act of an injured party who forgives; *to be reconciled* is the condition of one who has committed an offence and has obtained forgiveness. See Matthew 5:23, 24. "If thou bring thy gift to the altar, and there remember that thy brother hath ought against thee (hath ground of complaint against thee), leave there thy gift before the altar and go thy way; first be reconciled to thy brother (obtain his forgiveness), then come and offer thy gift."

God is in this passage represented as forgiving the world, as breathing out forgiveness generally through an atonement. Immediately after the fall, He had made known His purpose of restoring the lost race through the instrumentality of a descendant of the woman who should accomplish His object at the cost of a temporary suffering to Himself. In the fullness of time, the Deliverer came forth, and He was declared to be no less than the only begotten of the Father and the manifestation and expression of His nature, full of grace and truth. By the appointment of the Father, He became a sin offering for the sins of the world. He is thus not only the proof and pledge of divine love but also a most appropriate organ through which that love may be dispensed to sinners in perfect accordance with the holiness of the divine government. God manifested

---

69. John 6:53.

in Christ, therefore, means God as the holy and gracious forgiver of sins. This is His attitude. All who see Him in this attitude must know and feel that they are pardoned, but sin hides the forgiving character of God from us, and the accusation of conscience raises a cloud between God and the sinner. The forgiving love of God being manifested through an atonement declares itself to be a consuming fire to evil, and thus no heart that does not sympathize with the threatened destruction of evil can possibly embrace cordially or enjoy fully the forgiveness of the gospel, and, therefore, as long as a man chooses to keep his sin, so long he refuses to receive the forgiving love of God. In such circumstances, although God remains the same, although He is still the God of holy pardon, yet the creature can have no real peace, no true sense of this forgiving love—and if it continues in that state through all eternity, it must through all eternity be a child of wrath and outer darkness. And therefore, when it pleases God to make the light of his reconciling countenance shine through these veils and clouds and obstacles, the man may be said to be then first pardoned, because he then first admits or accepts or feels the pardon. When one man loves another, that other is loved whether he accepts the love that is bestowed on him or not. And in like manner, when God in Christ forgives the world, the world is forgiven whether it accepts the pardon or not. And as in the first case, the refuser of human kindness receives no joy and no benefit from it, though it has been bestowed, so in the second case, those who understand not and see not and feel not God's pardon, receive no joy, no benefit from it, though it also has been bestowed. So, when the Savior came into the world, it is said of Him that "He came unto His own but His own received Him not; but as many as received Him, to them gave He the privilege of becoming sons of God, even to them who believed in His name."[70] He came to the *world*, and pardon was and is contained in Him. Those who receive him receive pardon in Him. Those who do not receive Him, do not receive pardon.

Let us now proceed to examine some of the texts that appear to represent pardon as a gift bestowed upon believing or upon being baptized. We may take the Acts of the Apostles and look over the chapters. Acts 2:38. "Then Peter said, repent and be baptized every one of you in the name of Christ, *for* the remission of sins." I think that any person acquainted with the original will agree with me in translating this verse

70. John 1:11–12.

differently.[71] It ought to be, Repent or rather change your minds and let every one of you be baptized into the doctrine of forgiveness of sins for Christ's sake. To be *baptized into a doctrine* is the ordinary phrase of the New Testament. The commission given to the Apostles in the end of St. Matthew's Gospel ought to be rendered "baptizing them (not *in*, but) *into*[72] the name of the Father, and the Son, and the Holy Ghost"; *that is*, introducing them into that manifestation of the divine character (for that is always the meaning of *name*) in which God reveals Himself as the restorer of fallen man through the atonement of the Son and the quickening of the Spirit. So, in Romans 6:3. "As many of us as were baptized into Jesus Christ were baptized into His death" that is, were baptized into the doctrine that He died for sinners. I do not indeed think that the passage that has been quoted from the Acts can with justice be made to bear any other sense than that which I have now given it, [in other words,][73] "let every one of you be baptized into that doctrine that teaches the forgiveness of sins in the name or through the work of Christ"; *that is*, into a truth as unchangeable as God but in these latter days manifested in Jesus Christ. The Greek preposition (*ĕis*), which belongs to "the forgiveness of sins," and not that one (*epi*) that precedes "the name of Jesus Christ," is the preposition that in the Greek Testament usually indicates the direct object of baptism, and thus even attention to grammatical accuracy will conduct us to the conclusion that the true rendering is "baptized into the forgiveness of sins for the sake of Christ" and not "in the name of Christ, for the forgiveness of sins."[74]

Acts 3:19. "Repent ye therefore and be converted, that your sins may be blotted out—when the times of refreshing shall come from the presence of the Lord; and He shall send Jesus Christ, which before was preached unto you." Leave, therefore, your false notions of God and be converted to that true view of his character that blots out sin and assures of the forgiveness of sin—(as for the remaining part of the passage, Schleusner's[75] interpretation seems to be very satisfactory)—"especially now

71. Erskine is about to argue for a literal rendering of the New Testament Greek text, which instead of saying "*for* the forgiveness of sins" reads "*into* the forgiveness of sins."

72. Strong's 1519 *ĕis* into.

73. Replaced "viz."

74. For additional support for Erskine's way of translating Acts 2:38, see "In the name" in Vincent's *Word Studies in the New Testament*, vol. I, 149.

75. Johann Friedrich Schleusner (1759–1831) was considered one of the more

that the times of refreshing have come from the presence of the Lord, and that he hath sent Jesus Christ, who was before promised by the prophets."

That this interpretation of the latter clause is correct appears to me quite evident from the fact that it is the first and not the second coming of our Lord that is here referred to for—His second coming is separately mentioned in the 21st verse. But the first coming was past when this was spoken. The times of refreshing here spoken of, therefore, were the gospel times merely or the times intervening between the first and second coming of Christ, and the forgiveness of sin or the sense of forgiveness belongs to these times and is not deferred till the next dispensation as our translation seems to indicate. Forgiveness is surely not a future thing.

Acts 10:43. "To Him give all the prophets witness, that whosoever believeth on Him shall through His name receive the remission of sins." The word *receive* here has the same sense that it has in John 1:12, which has been already quoted, "He came to his own, and His own received Him not," or accepted Him not. He had come to them whether they had received Him or not and had the remission of sin, but those only who believed in his true character, viz. that He had come as a destroyer of the works of the devil and a propitiation for the sins of the world, would in that very character of Him read and receive their own forgiveness.

The next passage that I quote is still more distinct on this subject. Acts 13:38, 39. "Be it known unto you therefore, men and brethren, that through this man is preached unto you the forgiveness of sins; and by Him all that believe are justified from all things from which ye could not be justified by the law of Moses." Here the forgiveness is declared to be universal, but the justification is limited to those who believe. The pardon is given to all, it is laid down at every door, but those only who receive it, those only who believe in the unspeakable gift are justified—they only have their consciences purged of guilt and are delivered from the burden of unpardoned sin.

And I cannot but think that Abram's justification was nothing other than a sense of acceptance arising out of a belief in the general promises of God. In the 12th chapter of Genesis, we read that God had said to Abraham, "Get thee out of thy country, and from thy kindred, and from thy father's house, unto a land that I will show thee; and I will make of thee a great nation; and in thee shall all the families of the earth

---

prominent German theological scholars in Erskine's day.

be blessed."[76] Abram had surely heard before this time that a deliverer had been promised to the lost race of Adam, whether it had made any impression on his heart or not, and he would now understand that this deliverer was to be his own descendant according to the flesh. Induced by this promise, Abraham went forth as a stranger and pilgrim on the earth, but still his mind does not seem to have been quite satisfied that the promise was to be fulfilled for we find that when God appeared to him some time after and said to him, "I am thy shield and exceeding great reward,"[77] he expressed a general distrust. "And Abram said, Behold to me thou hast given no seed, and lo! One born in mine house is mine heir."[78] Upon this God renews the promise. "And He brought him forth abroad, and said, Look now towards heaven, and tell the stars if thou be able to number them; and He said unto him, So shall thy seed be."[79] And then it is added, "And he believed in the Lord, and He counted it to him for righteousness."[80] Now, if we suppose that God rewarded the greatness of Abram's confidence in Him by accepting him and freeing him from guilt, then we must also suppose that pardon is no more of grace but of debt. And if we decline this interpretation as being contrary to the whole tenor of the gospel, what other explanation can we adopt but that which has been suggested, [that is to say][81] that from the greatness of God's kindness manifested in his promises to him, Abraham was led to infer his acceptance with Him and to look to Him with confidence. It was not by the belief of any direct promise or declaration of pardon to himself personally that he was thus justified, but by the belief of a promise evidently renewing and confirming a former promise that bore that in him all the families of the earth should be blessed or that the expected deliverer in whom the world was to be blessed should descend from him. All that he had indistinctly heard or understood of the promised bruiser of the serpent seemed now explained to him and realized by him. He looked forward to the day of the deliverer, and as that deliverer Himself said of him, he saw it and was glad.[82]

76. Gen 12:1–3.

77. Gen 15:1.

78. Gen 15:3.

79. Gen 15:5.

80. Gen 15:6.

81. Replaced "viz."

82. John 8:56.

Abram believed in the Lord, in the purposed mercy of the Lord, and He counted it to him for righteousness. He *reasoned it* unto him—He taught him to argue from it his own acceptance. Now it was not written for his sake only that this inference was reasoned into him, but for our sakes also that we may know from God's own word that it was a fully warranted inference that he thus drew from the general promise of the deliverer, and that we are warranted to draw the same inference from the revealed fact that the Father has given the Son to death as a propitiation for our sins and has raised Him again in proof that the propitiation was accepted.[83] Being therefore justified by this belief—having our consciences freed from the weight of unpardoned sin by the belief of this accepted atonement, we have peace with God, through our Lord Jesus Christ.[84] See Genesis 12 and 15 and Romans 4 and 5. I do not see in what other way this transaction and the passages referring to it can be explained unless we have recourse to the idea of faith being rewarded as a meritorious work by acceptance with God.

The reader may apply the principles of explanation that have been now given to any other passages of the same character.

We shall now consider some passages of another character—such as, "believe in the Lord Jesus Christ, and thou shalt be saved."[85] "He that believeth in Him shall not perish, but have everlasting life."[86] With regard to such passages, I have to observe at the outset, that salvation and eternal life are things quite different from pardon. Salvation is the healing of the spiritual diseases of the soul, and eternal life is the communication of the life of God to the soul. These things are done for and in the soul of man by the knowledge of God entering into him and abiding in him and giving him a participation in the divine nature. This saving knowledge is contained in the doctrine of the forgiveness of sins through the atonement of Christ, and this knowledge can only enter into him by being believed. This doctrine, then, of the forgiveness of sins through Jesus Christ is the medicine and nourishment of the soul—faith is taking this medicine and feeding on this nourishment—salvation and sanctification and heaven and eternal life are different names for spiritual health and strength and enjoyment, which are the blessed effects of this spiritual medicine and

---

83. Rom 4:25—Jesus our Lord "was handed over to death for our trespasses and was raised for our justification" (NRSV).

84. Rom 5:1.

85. Acts 16:31.

86. John 3:16.

this spiritual nourishment. So "believe in the Lord Jesus Christ and thou shalt be saved" is not a nostrum nor a magical amulet but a description of the way to spiritual health. The Philippian jailer had been arrested by the voice of Paul when in the very act of plunging into eternity. He now looked back on what had happened with the feelings of a man who in the morning contemplates the full extent of a danger through which he had passed unconsciously during the night—he lived the danger over again and felt the fear. His arm had been stopped, and his life saved by the voice of one of these prisoners whom he had thrust into the inner prison. He must have known that it was for preaching a new religion that these prisoners had been committed to him by the magistrates with a special charge of safe custody, and he knew that he had not softened his charge in the execution of it. It was a remarkable night. Nature, or the God of nature, seemed to take part with the prisoners and to protest against the wrong done to them. There was a great earthquake so that the foundations of the prison were shaken—all the doors were opened, and everyone's bands were loosed, and then when he was about to kill himself supposing that the prisoners were fled, he was saved by the voice of one of these men assuring him that none had escaped. As his agitated mind hastily contemplated and compared these striking things, he seems to have been led to connect them all with the new God whose claims and authority these men had been asserting. And surely the Spirit of that God had spoken in the agony of his soul and in his felt nearness to the unseen eternity and had revealed to him the solitary helplessness and emptiness of his heart and had thus awakened his desire after a satisfying good not under the dominion of change and death and had thus caused him to open his mouth wide that it might be filled. Under these impressions, he came trembling and fell before Paul and Silas and said, "Sirs, what must I do to be saved?" And they said, "Believe on the Lord Jesus Christ, and thou shalt be saved." And then it immediately follows that "they spake unto him the word of the Lord," that is, they explained to him the gospel—they told him who Jesus Christ was and what he had done for the salvation of men. This was absolutely necessary—for these words, "believe on the Lord Jesus Christ and thou shalt be saved," however full of meaning to one who knows the gospel, yet if spoken alone and without a commentary must have been absolutely unintelligible to a Macedonian jailer who knew nothing at all about Jesus Christ. Pressed by his fears, he might have answered to such an address, "I will believe anything," but would this have been receiving the message of Him who teaches man knowledge, or could he have been enlightened or benefited in any way by such a faith or rather such a superstitious credulity? Paul must have told him that the God of heaven and earth, the Holy One who cannot look upon iniquity, *yet* looks with a father's love on this lost world[87]—yes, that He has so loved them as to give His Son as a propitiation for their sins—that Jesus Christ is this Son—the image of the invisible God, the manifestation of His holy love, and that through His atonement a full and free forgiveness is proclaimed to every man, and the access of God as to a loving father and a hearer of prayer is laid open to every man. We may suppose the jailer then asking, "but is there anything that I have to do in order to entitle me to a participation in these privileges and blessings?" And Paul answers,

> No, nothing. All that you have to do is immediately to use them and enjoy them. If you believe this history of God's love in providing so costly an atonement for the sins of the whole world, you will not doubt of His forgiveness to yourself—you will know that wherever you are, you have an Almighty friend who will never leave you and never forsake you—you will ask him and he will give you living water that will bathe your heart with gladness and purify you even as He is pure. "Believe on the Lord Jesus Christ, and thou shalt be saved."

Perhaps some of my readers may think that the observation that I am now going to make is frivolous or overfine, but I am myself persuaded that it is deeply important, and I beg their attention to it. I think that much obscurity has arisen from considering these words, "believe in the Lord Jesus Christ, and thou shalt be saved," as a statement of the gospel. If the gospel really consists in this proclamation, "believe in the Lord Jesus Christ, and thou shalt be saved," then to believe the gospel is "to believe that those who believe in the Lord Jesus Christ shall be saved." Well, then, I believe that those who believe in the Lord Jesus Christ shall be saved—the question then comes to be, "do I believe in the Lord Jesus Christ myself?" If I do, I am saved; if I do not, I am not saved. Then comes a doubt, "Have I any evidence of the sincerity of my faith?" Surely, I have

---

87. A reference to Hab 1:13. It was common in Erskine's day to quote only the first part of this verse to support the teaching that God cannot abide sinners. On the contrary, Erskine is saying that God is a loving Father whose arms are open wide to all His children. Habakkuk, after praying, "O LORD my God, you are the Holy One. Your eyes are too pure to behold evil and to look on iniquity" continues in essence with the question, "So why do you?" reversing the initial thought.

been very unfaithful to my light. It is quite clear that the mind cannot find firm footing in this way. It is an unravelable perplexity. But suppose the inquirer says, "Yes, I am sure that I believe in the Lord Jesus Christ," I only observe, that if he draws his hope from this fact of his believing, he is as far from the spirit of the gospel as the man who rests his hope on his alms-deeds. Whenever my own faith is the source of my comfort, I am sure that I have an empty cistern to draw from. It is not in the nature of things that I should be able to draw peace or strength or holiness from knowing that I believe a fact, however true and important that fact may be. The fact itself may be a comfort to me, but my knowing that I believe the fact cannot he a comfort to me. The gospel is not "he that believeth shall he saved," but it is "God gave His Son to be a propitiation for the sins of the whole world." Let the reader leisurely compare these two statements and judge between them according to the word of God. If the first statement be the true gospel, then the gospel consists simply in a promise to faith. If the second be the true gospel, then the gospel consists in a manifestation of the unutterable love of God to sinners of mankind. The belief of the first is a belief that a promise has been made to faith, and therefore none can draw comfort from it except those who are *sure* that they have the true faith. The belief of the second is a belief that God forgives sinners for the sake of Christ, and this will give comfort to anyone who knows that he is a sinner. I hope that I have made my meaning clear for the error that I am opposing seems to me very general and a great source of disquietude. Are there not many who when seeking for peace inquire rather "have I believed?" than "hath God indeed made a propitiation for the sins of the whole world?" Yet surely this is the question, and blessed be God, the answer is an unchangeable answer resting on the unchangeableness of God and not vacillating according to the high or low spirits of a weak mortal. "God hath given His Son to be a propitiation for the sins of the whole world,"[88] and through that propitiation "He is blotting out transgression and no longer remembering sin."[89] This is his name forever, "and they who know His name will put their trust in Him, for He never faileth them that seek Him."[90]

88. 1 John 2:2; 4:10.

89. Isa 43:25.

90. Ps 9:10.

This name of God is the strong tower into which the righteous flees and is safe.[91] Oh, reader! Are you in this strong tower? How would you feel if it were now said to thee by a voice that you could not mistake nor gainsay, "This night thy soul shall be required of thee?" Oh, my brother! your God has given His Son for you to be a propitiation for your sins. He has said, "Look unto Me and be saved[92]—Come unto Me, and I will give thee rest."[93] The love from which these gifts and promises and words of kindness flow is the strong tower. Will you not flee into it? And if you cannot—if your evil heart of unbelief will not allow you—will you not cry to Him who made your heart, and who can make it new, and ask Him to lead you into this strong tower? For, oh! it is the one thing needful. That tower is the secret place of the Most High, the shadow of the Almighty. If you are there, although you have no earthly friend nor refuge nor comfort, yet you are rich, for nothing shall separate you from the love of God that is in Christ Jesus, and if you are not there, you are an outcast and a beggar although all the crowns of the earth were at your foot. Cry, then, unto Him and take no rest until He conducts you in there—though you have until now received the grace of God in vain, that grace is still lying at your door and begging for admittance. Fear not, therefore, to ask and [be not remiss].[94] Open your mouth wide, and he will fill it. And let no one be alarmed by the description of those who flee into this tower. They are called the "righteous," but this means no more than what is said of them in the other passage—"*they that know Thy name* shall put their trust in Thee."[95] They that know that the name of God is merciful and gracious, forgiving iniquity, transgression, and sin[96] through the atonement of Christ. They that know that this is His *name* will put their trust in Him. They will flee into this *name* as their refuge and hiding place and strong tower. They are the righteous. They are justified or delivered from fear and distrust of God on account of unpardoned sin by their knowledge of this name of God according to that word in Isaiah, "By the knowledge of Himself shall my righteous servant justify many, for He shall bear their

---

91. Prov 18:10.

92. Isa 45:22.

93. Matt 11:28.

94. Replaced "slack not."

95. Ps 9:10.

96. Exod 34:6–7.

iniquities."[97] He lets them know that He has borne their iniquities, and thus, they are justified. And thus is the spirit of childlike dependence revived in them and sustained in them. This is the manna that is daily rained round all our habitations. This is the feast of fat things to which we are all bidden. Oh, reader! Lift up your heart unto the Lord and say, "Blessed be Thy glorious name for ever, and let the whole earth be filled with Thy glory—Amen and Amen."[98] And oh! heed to thyself that thou neglect not this great salvation and beware lest you convert the blessing into a curse by slighting it or refusing it. It is not a vain thing. It is your life. If you would grow for heaven, you must live upon this food—nothing else will do.

"This is life eternal, to know Thee, the only true God and Jesus Christ, whom Thou hast sent."[99] Eternal life is not given as a premium for knowing God. The knowledge of God as revealed in Christ is eternal life. God is light and the knowledge of God is a ray of that light. It is an emanation of God, and the soul into which it enters becomes a partaker of the divine nature. We may have an atheistical knowledge of God and of Christianity, as I have before observed—that is, we may receive the doctrines without receiving the God of the doctrines, just as the philosophers of this world receive the doctrines of natural science without thinking of receiving the God of nature, or as men are continually receiving the events of life without receiving God who manifests himself in them. And therefore, it is most necessary to bear continually on our minds that it is God that we have to do with and not a science. The most important truth with regard to the doctrines of revelation is that they are the manifestations of that ever present Almighty God in whose hand our breath is and whose are all our ways. These doctrines are lights merely to guide us to God, and if they serve not this purpose, they serve no purpose. They are channels through which that spirit might to be received into the heart, and if they bring not this spirit, they do nothing.

Selling All for the Pearl of Great Price

Christianity has two fields. The one is the infinite and unchangeable character of God—the other is the heart of man. The first is all light—original,

97. Isa 53:11.

98. Ps 72:19.

99. John 17:3.

uncreated light. The second, in itself, is all darkness—but it is created with the capacity of receiving light. The great object of Christianity is to dispel the darkness of the second field by introducing into it the light of the first.

Man may know that there is light in God's field, and he may know something of the color and the qualities of the rays of that light, and yet he may be unvisited by a single ray. He may know about it as a man naturally blind may know about material light. And all the while, though he reasons about it, he has it not—he is in darkness. But why is the heart of man dark? Surely it was not so when God pronounced it good. No, it was then light, but it was light merely and solely because it was open to receive the light of God. The creature is all darkness when separated from the Creator—when shut against Him, and man has separated himself from God and shut out his light—and never can he have light again until he opens his heart to receive the light of God. As easily may the eye create light for itself independent of the sun as the soul of man create light for itself independent of God. There is no light for a soul but in God. If He is not in you, the light that is in you is darkness.

The natural sun entering upon the polar regions that have been locked up in the death and frost and darkness of their long winter and filling all things with light and life and warmth is but a feeble emblem of the entrance of the sun of righteousness on the cold and dead and dark regions of the human heart. It is a land of darkness, as darkness itself inhabited by lies and vain imaginations and lying under the shadow of death. It is a chaos and a terror to itself whenever it can look upon itself. But no sooner does that sun enter—no sooner does the dead heart drink his quickening beams, but it revives. It finds that the light is life—the darkness and the fear and the frozen death are past—there is a new principle of life imparted. The cold and torpid heart begins to open its rigid and shrunken veins to receive the life blood and the quickening spirits that flow from Him who is the heart and the head of the spiritual universe. It finds that that light is love and that that uncreated and embracing and omnipotent love is its joyful and satisfying portion through all eternity. "Surely the light is sweet, and a pleasant thing it is for the eyes to behold the sun."[100]

Each revealed perfection of God as it enters the heart of man goes to form a part of the Christian character and is necessary to the filling up

---

100. Eccl 11:7.

of that character. The full character is a cordial and delighted and intelligent sympathy with the whole will of God. But we must know God in order thus to sympathize with Him for we cannot sympathize with what we know not and believe not. We may know and believe many things without sympathizing with them, but no man can know or believe in God without sympathizing with Him. For he that does not know God as the light and the life and the portion of his soul, knows not God, and he that knows this cannot but sympathize with Him. This full sympathy, then, is the full receiving of the revealed will and thoughts and purposes of God. It is the casting out of self to make room for God. It is the being cut off from our own root, and the being grafted on the root of God. It is the spirit of affectionate dependence.

"This is life eternal, to know Thee, the only true God, and Jesus Christ, whom Thou hast sent"[101]—that is, to know God as revealed in Christ—to know Him in His relation to sinners. It is to know His purpose of destroying the works of the devil through the work of the Redeemer. It is to know the tenderness of His love and the freeness of it. It is to know Him as the prodigal knew his father when he felt his arms about him, and it is at the same time to know, that the grand object of this love is the eradication of evil.

And "this is life eternal," says the faithful and true witness. It is a living principle then and not a mere notion. It is a participation of the life of God. It is an indwelling of the Spirit of God. He is the fountain of eternal life, and there is no other fountain. The Savior complained, "Ye will not come unto Me, that ye might have life."[102] There was but one life and one dispenser of that life in the whole universe, yet they would not come to Him for it. Oh! if they had known the gift of God, and who it was that offered it to them, they would have asked, and He would have given them eternal life.

Life eternal does not consist in knowing that there is a God and that there is a Savior, but in knowing God and in knowing the Savior as a child knows his father, as a friend knows his friend. When man discovers that his Creator, the fountain of eternity, the fountain of his being and of all being in whom and by whom he lives and thinks and feels—who pervades and sustains his soul and his body in all their parts—whoever is and ever must be essentially present in every faculty and capacity of his

101. John 17:3.

102. John 5:40.

nature without whom nothing lives, nothing happens, nothing is done through all worlds—in whom as in their one root all the varieties of things are united and from whom as from their one root, they all grow—when he discovers that this great one, this mystery that contains and binds in and animates the universe, has a love for him passing thought as well as utterance, a love that led Him to take on Himself the human nature that He might suffer and groan and die for him—when he discovers that He did this that he might live forever in the knowledge and fellowship of His holy love, dwelt in by Him and animated by His Spirit and filled with His fullness with His light and love and joy—Oh! then the darkness is past and the true light is come. He has found the pearl of eternity, the pearl of great price. He knows the meaning of that word, "he that hath the Son hath life."[103] He has found the pearl, and for joy thereof, he goes and sells all that he has and buys it.[104]

But he must sell all that he has in order to possess this pearl. Nothing less than all will serve. And yet the pearl is a free gift. What then is meant by saying that the merchantman who had found it went and sold all that he had and bought it? The meaning is that there is no room for it in a heart that is occupied by other things—and he who would possess it must make room for it. It is not and cannot be enjoyed unless it fill the heart. It must be the first and the last, the object of the thoughts and the affections and the desires. The pearl of great price is eternal life—it is the love of God reigning in the heart. It is the being grafted onto the true vine. Now eternal life has no fellowship with sensual, selfish, worldly life, and the love of God cannot reign in the heart while *self* still reigns there disposing of the affections according to its own will, and the soul cannot he grafted on the true vine unless it be first cut off from its own root. All, therefore, that we have to sell is *self*, and this must be sold before we can possess the pearl. While self remains, we may hear of God by the hearing of the ear—we may read and reason and talk about Him—we may have our feelings and imaginations strongly excited by the ideas that we have formed of Him—but He is not *our* God, He is not the portion of our souls. There is no room for Him there just as there was no room for Him in the inn when He was born into our nature and our world. Yet let no one think that his business is first to cast out self and then to look for this pearl. The knowledge of the value of the pearl is the instrument in the

103. 1 John 5:12.
104. Matt 14:36.

hand of God by which self, the strong man armed, is cast out, and it is the only instrument. They that know the *name* of God will put their trust in Him—and they who know the value of the pearl will sell all that they have and buy it. But they that know not the *name* of God cannot trust in Him, and they that know not the value of the pearl cannot part with anything so dear as *self* in order to make room for it. They keep self, and in keeping self, they refuse the pearl. Is *self*, then, yet reigning in us? Let us not deceive ourselves by vain words. We have yet neither part or lot in the matter, and our religion is nothing other than Simon's traffic who would have purchased the Holy Ghost to flatter and pamper self.[105] While we continue thus, we are strangers to the covenant of promise—we are without home or hope or God in the world. But the love of God is still lying at our door, and the ear of God is still open to our cry, and the sighing of the prisoner comes before Him. He waits to be gracious, and He delights in mercy. Yet is the danger imminent for every hour of delay strengthens self and confirms the opposition of the heart against God. Let us consider how we shall estimate the pearl when we come to die, and how we shall estimate self—Oh! we know well that at that hour we shall be ready to give ten thousand times ten thousand worlds if we had them for one smile of the face of God, for one good hope of eternal life. And if such a smile and such a hope be worth so much at that hour, why should they be worth less at this hour? *At this hour*, reader—for can you say what an hour may bring forth? Can you assure yourself that you have an hour to live? There are thousands at this moment within an hour of death, and of these there are many who have no more thought of it than you have. And certainly, your hour is not far off—and then comes eternity. Oh! then is there any madness equal to the madness of neglecting the soul and the favor of God and spending your short uncertain hour here in treasuring up for yourself regrets and fears against the hour of death and misery for the life to come? Is it not madness in an immortal being to leave eternity entirely out of his account of existence when, in truth, it is the only thing in his existence that is worth thinking of? Neglect not the pearl for it is a pearl of *great price*—it is the immortal life and health and hope of the soul, and what shall a man give in exchange for his soul? We must have such a religion as will stand by us at the hour of death and prepare us for our Lord's summons, else we may as well be without a religion. We must have a religion that will cast out self and that will make us hasten unto the

105. The story of Simon the sorcerer is found in Acts 8.

day of Christ and long for his appearing and conform us to his likeness. Such a religion and such a religion alone is the pearl of great price—the one thing needful for a sinner.

Oh! that we felt its value and the freeness and the fullness of the love which presses it on our acceptance, and that our hearts would open to receive it! But even when all this is in some degree felt, the evil is that the heart tries to make it its *own* work—it does not like to be a mere receiver, and this introduction of self shuts the door. Hence it is that many are called, but few chosen. Many hear the message and are glad to hear of a deliverance from pain and sorrow and death, but when they find that self must be cast out before this deliverance can come in, by and bye they are offended. The happiness of *self* and the happiness of *God* are two structures that cannot stand together for there are materials in the heart only for one, and, therefore, to build the one, the other must be pulled down. This is what the natural man cannot receive. This is work for Him who made us, and before God gives the pearl to any man, He lets him feel well that the acquisition of it is not his own work. He shuts in all under unbelief that all may feel themselves mere dependents upon mercy—sovereign mercy.[106]

We know that God is love, and that His thoughts toward a man have been thoughts of love from everlasting. But His dispensations in the meantime are far above, out of our sight. How is it that one is made a partaker of eternal life, and that another goes on in willful blindness to the grave? He does not give an account of His doings. Let us humble ourselves in the dust before Him—we are of yesterday and know nothing. The Judge of all the earth will do right. But this we can understand that at each door he has laid down the gift of his Son and in Him the gift of all things. To each creature He has given the privilege of prayer and the promise of the Spirit to those who ask Him of that Spirit who will open the heart to receive and understand the gift of the Savior and thus restore the prodigal to his place in his Father's house.

The appeals that God makes to every man through the occasional misgivings of conscience and the appointments of providence and especially through that sense of the weariness and unsatisfactoriness and hopelessness of life that forces itself upon him when he is not under the immediate exciting influence of some particular object are all urgent invitations to prayer and to seek that good from the Creator that has in

---

106. An allusion to Romans 11:32 (King James Version). "For God hath concluded them all in unbelief, that He might have mercy on all."

vain been sought from the creature. Why is the world such a scene as it is? Why is life such a scene? Think for a moment of the loathsome sin and the loathsome misery that cover the crowded populations of our cities and overspread in many instances immense regions of the earth. It is a festering and putrefying evil that defies all human skill and power and benevolence to cure. And think of the better regulated sin and the better disguised misery that poison the more decent or the more refined portions of the species. The bitter root of all this is that self has taken the place of God in man's heart. And thus, there is no common center by which man might be united to each other for all follow each man his own *self,* and there are as many centers as there are individuals. And there is no true order in the individual any more than in the mass for the keystone of the mind is gone. For the only common center of men is God, and love to Him is the only common principle that can unite them to each other. And as God is the common center of the whole moral world, so he is the keystone of the arch in each individual mind. And thus the "fool who hath said in his heart there is no God"[107] has chosen as his portion a restless misery within and a tumultuous strife without. Is not this man's state in the world? Where can we turn for hope and consolation in such circumstances but unto our Creator. Our revolt from Him is the very spring and source of the evil, and our cure lies only in our return to Him. Oh! that each heart might hear and answer to that voice, "Return unto Me, for I have redeemed you."[108] "Look unto Me, and be ye saved all the ends of the earth."[109] We must look; we must believe; we must receive the truth of God, otherwise we cannot be saved. Not that looking at or believing or receiving any thing is rewarded by salvation, but because God is truth and in order to receive God into our souls, we must receive the truth. God knocks at our door under the form of the truth. He comes near to us in the manifestation of His love and the proclamation of a pardon. But a pardon unreceived can no more save the soul than a medicine unreceived can cure the body. The light may shine without, but if the eyes be shut against it, all within is darkness. Salvation does not consist in the removal of a penalty or punishment, but in dying unto self and living unto God—in being made one with the Father and the Son—in having one mind, one will, one spirit with God. Salvation is

107. Ps 53:1.

108. Isa 44:22.

109. Isa 45:22.

the truth of God abiding richly and efficiently in the soul, and how can truth enter the heart but by being believed? Salvation is thus by faith and by faith alone, that is, it is the effect produced on the heart by the truth of God believed. Sanctification and salvation are all one, and the great high priest prays thus—"Sanctify them through Thy truth; Thy word is truth."[110] Knowledge is truth in the understanding. Sanctification is truth in the will and the affections. It is choosing and estimating and loving things according to truth, and it can enter the will and the affections only through the understanding. Therefore, it is that souls are sanctified only through truth. And Christianity is just truth for there is nothing *arbitrary* in Christianity.

We are not called upon to believe anything merely for the sake of be-lieving it or merely in obedience to the command of a being more power-ful than ourselves and on whose will our happiness depends. Christianity explains the true relationship between the Creator and the creature—it ascribes the evil that is in the world to the breach of that relationship on the part of the creature, and it declares the means by which God purposes to heal the breach and to bring out of this foul stain a higher manifesta-tion of His own character and a higher holiness and happiness to the restored race as well as to all the rest of the spiritual family. The intelligent belief of these things is the way by which we may enter into sympathy with the mind and will and purposes of God, and thus it is that faith is the natural and necessary way by which man is to be reunited to God, for reunion with God and a renewed sympathy with His will and purposes are one and the same thing.

Jesus' Prayer

The great high priest prays, "Sanctify them through Thy truth; Thy word is truth."[111] The truth is the instrument, but it is the God of the truth who works. In fact, the "word" is not truth to our souls unless God be perceived in it. While it lies in our minds as a mere knowledge or system of theology, it is of no profit to us—it is a body without a soul, not that it is so in itself, but it is so to us so long as we do not make it a channel of communion with God. If we would have our souls really fed by the word, we must get it fresh from the mouth of God Himself, and we must get it

110. John 17:17.

111. John 17:17.

daily for like the manna in the wilderness, it will not keep. We must receive it in the spirit of dependence. We must ask for it till He gives it—we must open our mouths wide till He fills them. "Sanctify them through Thy truth," thus our high priest prayed and prays without ceasing, and it is sweet when the soul is dry and comfortless and cannot pray with any fervor of feeling to sit down at His feet and say amen to His prayer. And oh! what high things will the soul hear that sits there, and with what high things will its amen mingle? Hear some of them—

> Neither pray I for these alone, but for them also which shall believe on Me through their word that they all may be one; as thou, Father, art in Me, and I in Thee, that they also may be one in Us. And the glory which thou gavest Me, I have given them; that they may be one, even as We are one. I in them, and thou in Me; that they may be made perfect in one.

"Father, I will that they also whom Thou hast given me be with Me where I am, that they may behold My glory," and "that the love wherewith Thou hast loved Me may be in them, and I in them."[112] He who prays thus is He whom the Father hears always—it is He who is the head over all things to His church. Will not the soul that hears this say with David, "who am I, and what is my house? and what can I say more unto thee? yet now, O LORD God, Thou art that God, and Thy words are true, and Thou hast promised this goodness unto Thy servant and now, O LORD God, the word that Thou hast spoken concerning Thy servant, establish it for ever, and do as Thou hast said."[113]

It is very profitable and delightful to read the Psalms in this same spirit, regarding them as the confessions and prayers, and praises and hopes and assurances that the great high priest presents to the Father in the name of His church. The soul that joins in this worship of the upper sanctuary must pray with confidence—it cannot doubt of an answer—it knows that it has the petitions that it asks because it asks according to the will of God and through the mouth of the all-prevailing Intercessor. This is indeed profitable for the soul for thus it learns a holy familiarity with heaven—it becomes one of that great multitude that no man can number—and as it sees and feels more of the privilege of being united to Christ and to His body, it learns more and more to loathe the contractedness and littleness of self and individuality and to pant after a full

112. John 17:20–26.

113. 2 Sam 7:18, 20, 28, 25.

participation in that free spirit that is the Spirit of God and the quickening breath of the universal family.

Perhaps some of my readers as they look back on the views that I have been laying before them may refer me at once to this very 17th chapter of John from which I have been making these most comforting quotations as a complete refutation of all that I have said on the universality of the love of God and of the pardon through the sacrifice of Christ. For in that prayer, our Lord only prays for such as either were then or should afterwards become believers. But there is no inconsistency here. The circumstances of the disciples at the time, and the character of the prayer itself fully explain the limitations in it. The disciples were at that moment, without knowing it, on the very brink of a most tremendous event that was to shake all their high hopes of their master's success and that was at first sight to appear the complete triumph of the world over his cause. He had all along been forewarning them of this event, and particularly as it came near its accomplishment, but their eyes were [held fast][114] so that they should not see the truth, yet still he continued to prepare them for it. He had already distinctly told them that He was to suffer at the feast that was just about to be celebrated, and now He has recourse to another mode of encouragement and consolation. He prays in their hearing for them to the Father—and in His prayer he speaks as the high priest over the house of God above, and thus he draws their thoughts and expectations past the present sorrow and fixes them on that future triumph and glory that should be the consequence of His sufferings and that should be for a praise and a rest and a joy to His people forever and ever. They were soon to stand in need of a very special and very strong consolation, and so He gave it them. He let them know that He bore their individual names on His heart before His Father. They were soon to see Him crucified by the world, and thence learn to dread the world as their own enemy. He therefore prayed for them as distinct from the world, and that they might be kept from the evil that is in the world. They had heard that He had come to seek and to save the lost, but they needed in this their extremity something more precise, more exclusive, more directly applicable to themselves and to none other, and He did not withhold it from them. He therefore began his intercession with a prayer for them individually, but He did not end it so. He proceeded as high priest to embrace all who should afterwards believe on Him through their word, and by doing this,

---

114. Replaced archaic word "holden."

He gave to His their little flock an assurance that their numbers should be increased at the same time that He bequeathed an enduring consolation to all who at any period of the world should put their trust in Him. He does not then appear in this prayer as the Savior of sinners or as the propitiation for the sins of the whole world but as the elder brother of His disciples and as the head and high priest over the church of God. All are invited to come into the temple, and the access is open to all, but the high priest intercedes only for those who enter. The names and titles of Christ are all relative. He is the *shepherd* of His *sheep*; He is the *head* of His *body*; He is the *Savior* of *sinners;* He is the *propitiation* for the sins of *the world*. He came to seek and to save the lost. He came not to call the righteous but sinners to repentance. He invites all to come into the temple, but those who do not listen to His call remain without, lost in the death of sin. They enter not into the church of Christ. He is neither their head nor high priest. They have no part in His intercession. While those who do listen to Him, and whose hearts are opened to receive His message of love, do in that very message receive a new life that love becomes their life—they become members of his body and partakers of that divine life of which the fountain is in Him. He is their head and representative with the Father, and as He is their righteousness, so He is their intercessor. He is not the righteousness of those who do not believe in Him—and this not from His unwillingness, but because it is impossible—for He cannot be the confidence of those who do not confide in Him as he cannot be the nourishment of those who do not feed on Him. So also, He is not the high priest of those who are not His people, who are not the members of His church and of His body, *because* He cannot be the organ of those who are not partakers of His life. He cannot present the prayers of those who do not pray nor the offerings of those who offer nothing. As the Savior of sinners, He says, "Come unto Me all ye that are weary and heavy laden, and I will give you rest."[115] And as the Savior also, He prays, "Father, forgive them, for they know not what they do."[116] But, as the high priest, He says, "I pray for them: I pray not for the world, but for those whom Thou hast given Me, for they are Thine, and all Mine are Thine, and Thine are Mine, and I am glorified in them."[117] He is their organ of communication with the Father. They are one with Him. Their life is wholly derived from

115. Matt 11:28.

116. Luke 23:34.

117. John 17:9–10.

Him. Their prayers are the breathings of His Spirit within them, and He presents them with acceptance before the Father. Let us not then lose the comfort or enjoyment of this prayer by supposing that it marks any limitation of the Savior's love. It does not belong to Him as the seeker and saver of the lost, but as the organ of those who are partakers of His life and the members of His body. Let the believer read it with great joy for it is now making in His behalf, and it is always heard and always answered, and let the unbeliever as he reads it compare his own hopes for time and for eternity with the hopes of the least of those who are prayed for in it, and let him be urged to flee from wrath and to take refuge in this ark of the covenant of love—this true temple of the living God, and let him know that he has but to admit that love of God that has been long knocking at the door of his heart in order to his being himself admitted within this sacred enclosure.

This sacred enclosure is the true ark, the true Zoar,[118] the true city of refuge, and its gates stand open continually to admit all who will be persuaded to come in, and there is no safety out of it. This is the strong habitation whereto we may continually resort. Reader, ponder the last words of the prayer—"O righteous Father, the world hath not known Thee, but I have known Thee, and these have known that Thou hast sent Me; and I have declared unto them Thy name, and will declare it, that the love wherewith Thou hast loved Me, may be in them, and I in them."[119] You see that the great end and object of God's doings and Christ's sufferings for man is that the love of God, even that very love with which the Father loves the Son, may be in man and abide in him and unite him to God forever and ever. It was for this that Jesus Christ has declared, does declare, and will declare—the name of God—the holy love of God—the unwearied compassion of God. He declares this name of God that it may become a new life in man—a life [not subject][120] to sin or sorrow or death—a life that is nothing other than a stream flowing from and continually supplied from that eternal fountain of holy love that is in God. He does not declare this name that men may amuse themselves by talking about it or reasoning about it, but that they may be one with the Father and the Son. It is not by philosophy or speculation that we can know God but by the desire of the heart after Him, by the opening of the heart to

118. Gen 19:22–23, 30. Zoar was the place where Lot was told to take refuge while God rained brimstone and fire down on Sodom and Gomorrah.

119. John 17:25–26.

120. Replaced "unsubject" a word not found in modern dictionaries.

receive Him, by the spirit of prayer. Except you receive the kingdom of heaven as a little child, you shall in no wise enter therein.[121] There is no true religion except the holy love of God abiding in the heart, and there is no heresy so great as the want of it. God can only be known by love according to what the beloved disciple says, "he that loveth not, knoweth not God, for God is love."[122]

It is a question that I have often heard asked, "Do you think that the belief of such or such a doctrine or of such or such a view of a doctrine is essential to salvation?" This question always seems to me to indicate a mistake in the mind of the asker as to the nature of salvation. The heart that truly loves God as its good and its portion has got salvation, for salvation is the love of the heart for God. Any belief that produces this love is consistent with salvation, and any belief that does not and cannot produce this love is inconsistent with salvation. But let no one mistake. It is quite possible to love a God who after all may not be the true God but a mere idol of the imagination. God has told us Himself in His word what He is and what He has done so that we may know Him and love Him in His true character. If we love God for something that He is not—as for example, for a good-natured indifference whether His creatures are holy or not—we do not love God but a lie. A true knowledge of God is necessary to a true love of God as it is only a true love of God that can produce conformity to the true will of God in the heart of the creature. The evil, then, of taking up a wrong doctrine or a wrong view of a doctrine does not lie in this—that God punishes a man for not believing one thing more than another, but in this—that it interferes with the great purpose of religion, [that is][123] that the love of God and the Christ of God may abide in the heart of man conforming his mind and will to the mind and will of God.

"The world hath not known Thee, but I have known Thee."[124] Oh, infinite knowledge, the knowledge of the Father by the Son! But we may have our share in this wondrous knowledge. "No man knoweth the Son but the Father, neither knoweth any man the Father save the Son, and He to whomsoever the Son will reveal Him."[125] And the Son of God has de-

121. Mark 10:15; Luke 18:17.

122. 1 John 4:8.

123. Replaced "viz."

124. John 17:25.

125. Matt 11:27.

clared His Father's name and will declare it. He is standing and knocking at the door. We have not to ascend into the heaven nor to descend into the deep to find Him.[126] He is very near you, and He longs to reveal the Father to you and to give you that knowledge that is life eternal.

And it is through the Bible, read in the spirit of prayer, that He chiefly communicates this knowledge. "Thy word is truth."[127] This is our Urim and Thummim[128] that will tell us what is the mind of God in all things. We need not be ignorant of God's will or counsel while we have a Bible to consult. We often place much importance on having the advice of particular persons in whose judgment and friendship we have confidence, and we have great pleasure in asking and hearing their opinions. Alas! what can they tell us? What can they do for us? Why should we not go to God and consult Him rather? Reader, do you believe that the Bible is the word of God? and that God spoke it for this very purpose that by it He might direct and support and comfort man in his journey through time to eternity? And do you not need direction or support or comfort? And if you do, will you not go to the Bible to seek it? Where else can you expect it? We are so accustomed to the sight of a Bible that it ceases to be a miracle to us. It is printed just like other books, and so we forget that it is not just like other books. But there is nothing in the world like it or comparable to it. The sun in the firmament is nothing to it if it be really—what it assumes to be—an actual direct communication from God to man. Take up your Bible with this idea and look at it and wonder at it. It is a treasure of unspeakable value to you for it contains a special message of love and tender mercy from God to your soul. Do you wish to converse with God? Open it and read. And, at the same time, look to Him who speaks to you in it and ask Him to give you an understanding heart that you may not read in vain, but that the word may be in you as good seed in good ground bringing forth fruit unto eternal life. Only take care not to separate God from the Bible. Read it in the secret of God's presence and receive it from His lips and feed upon it, and it will be to you as it was to Jeremiah, the joy and rejoicing of your heart. The best advice that any one friend can give to another is to advise him to consult God, and the best turn that any book can do to its reader is to refer him to the Bible.

126. An allusion to Rom 10:6–8.

127. John 17:17.

128. A reference to Exod 28:30. The Urim and Thummin were two objects used by Israel's priests as instruments for discovering the divine will.

Let us seek to know more of the Bible, but in doing so, let us remember that however much we may add by study to our knowledge of the book, we have just so much true knowledge of God as we have love of Him and no more. Our continual prayer ought to be that our true notions may become true feelings, and that our orthodoxy and theology may become holy love and holy obedience. This is the religion of eternity, and the religion of eternity is the only religion for us—for yet a few days and we shall be in eternity.

Men are apt to think that religion is just one of the many duties of life, and that it ought to have its own time and its own place like the others—and they set apart for it churches and Sundays and certain other occasions—and having done so much for it, they seem to consider it an intruder if it appears out of these limits. Thus, we know that although the authority of God and the inspiration of the Bible are nominally acknowledged in this country, yet anyone who in the great deliberative assemblies of the nation, for instance, should quote the Bible as a reason for giving his vote one way or another would be generally regarded either as a fanatic or a canter [one who makes hypocritical pretensions to goodness]. The introduction of such a book or such an authority would be considered almost as great an impropriety as the introduction of a band of music. Now, religion is not just one of the many duties of life, it is itself a life. It is the taking a man off from his own root and grafting him on God as the new root of all his thoughts and desires and doings. And as the sap of the root circulates through every branch and twig and leaf of the tree—so the love of God that is the sap of this new spiritual root ought to circulate through every thought and desire and action of the man. If a man were truly religious, he would judge of everything by the light of God's will, and this will of God would be given as the reason of his judgment whenever he was asked for his reason. And amongst those who, *not nominally, but really* acknowledged the authority of God, such a reason would be considered as the only good reason that could be given. God is not really acknowledged in any country where His authority cannot be appealed to as a ground of judgment or of action without exciting astonishment. I mention this as a striking feature in the public character of the nation. The same men who would [reject scornfully][129] the mention of the Bible in one place would have no objections to it in another. They go to church and even to Bible and missionary societies perhaps. All

129. Replaced "scout."

that they insist on is that religion should keep its own plane. They know it only as a decency. They do not know it as the *great truth*—the paramount relation of their being—as that which according as it is present or absent determines the character of every thought, word, and action to be either right or wrong essentially.

Some Final Words

It is a small thing to me, says the Apostle of the gentiles, to be judged of you or of *man's day*.[130] The expression is remarkable—man's day. *This* is man's day. Man looks now at things and judges of them by the light of his own self-will, and his judgment passes current and is little questioned. But there is another day coming—the day of the Lord—and by the light of that day all the judgments of man's day shall be judged. Man's judgments shall pass away with man's day, but the judgment of the Lord shall stand for the day of the Lord is eternity. A man may live even here in the light of God's day, for many rays of that light are sent down into this world. There is much of it in the conscience. The Bible is full of it, and God answers prayer by the communications of it. And that light shows things as they are for it shows them as God sees them, and it shows things as they always will be for it is the light of eternity. That light shows God to be the only satisfying portion of the soul, and he who lives in that light chooses God for his portion. The light of man's day shows nothing but the perishing things of time as a portion, and he who lives in that light can choose no other portion. Now, judge of these two men as death approaches them. The one feels that in leaving this world he is leaving his portion and all that he knows or dreams of good forever. The other knows that he is going to the full enjoyment of his portion—of that portion that he has chosen here and tasted to be good, but which he cannot fully enjoy while he is encompassed with the body of his humiliation. To the one, all his thoughts are about to perish. To the other, all his thoughts are about to be accomplished.

So, life and death are set before every man. God makes a general proclamation of love and compassion to the whole race, and they who hear it rejoice for the consolation. He declares that Jesus Christ has been made a propitiation for the sins of the whole world, and He commands

---

130. 1 Cor 4:3 from Young's Literal Translation—"and to me it is for a very little thing that by you I may be judged, or by man's day, but not even myself do I judge."

all men to believe that their sins are atoned for by that propitiation, for John says that they who do not believe this make God a liar.[131] God proclaims over the whole world, "return unto Me ye backsliding children,"[132] and every one who hears His voice answers, "I will arise and go to my Father."[133] This love of God, this forgiveness, this invitation is universal and altogether independent of man's belief or unbelief, but it does man no good unless it enters into his heart and becomes the principle of a new life within him, and that it cannot do except it is believed. This proclamation of free unconditional mercy manifested in the gift of Christ to be a propitiation for the sins of the whole world is the blessed gospel of the grace of God—and it has "appeared unto all men, teaching us that denying ungodliness and worldly lusts, we should live godly, and righteously, and soberly in this present evil world, looking unto the blessed hope and glorious appearing of our great God and Saviour, Jesus Christ."[134]

The gospel is a message of free and unbounded love, and yet no message ever came to man that required him to make such sacrifices. But this is in the very nature of the thing. The receiver of a free and generous kindness cannot but feel himself required to answer it by the sacrifice of self, and he will refuse the kindness if he cannot make up his mind to the sacrifice. The heart that deliberately clings to *self* cannot for its very life receive or admit a generous and disinterested [free from selfish motive] kindness. If it does, it becomes itself generous—it must cast out self in order to admit the kindness. Its very baseness may enable it to receive an *act* of kindness, *a donation, an alms*, but it cannot receive the kindness without being changed into the same image. And so when the pardon of the gospel is viewed as a mere removal of penalties and as a deliverance from torments, a man may catch at the pardon and keep his selfishness, but when the pardon is seen to be a gift of infinite love, of holy, disinterested, self-sacrificing love on the part of God, laid down at the door of man's heart and waiting there with a patience that is grieved but not exhausted by the madly pertinacious rejection which it meets with—when it is seen to be the gift of God's heart, the gift of Himself to His poor prodigals, His apostate children—no man will catch at this pardon, no man will receive it or can receive it until he is prepared to sell all and buy

---

131. 1 John 5:10.

132. Jer 3:22.

133. Luke 15:18.

134. Titus 2:12–13.

it, until he is prepared to surrender himself and cast all out besides that he may make room for the reception of such an overwhelming, annihilating, unrepayable kindness. Such a love would be a perfect torture in the heart of any man who did not submit himself to it with a grateful humility, who did not recognize God as the only and necessary and perpetual giver and himself as nothing but a receiver.

The great practical difficulty is to realize these things. This love of God, this eternal embrace of the Father of our spirits, appears so glorious, so subduing, so attractive, that until by bitter experience we learn the deceitfulness of our own hearts, we can scarcely conceive the possibility of our ever forgetting God for a moment. But deep humiliation is the lesson that man must learn in this world. He is to be taught his own weakness and his incapacity to produce or maintain in himself the feeling of common gratitude to God without the continued supply of divine grace. He is to learn that he can be nothing but a receiver, that his strength consists in the strength of God communicated to him from moment to moment, that he has nothing of his own that is good *and never will have*, and that his spiritual perfection and blessedness consist in his being a receiver of God—of God's life and love and light—in his being a branch on the true vine and not a plant on his own root. Let him live in the spirit of dependence and the spirit of prayer and listen to that word, "Abide in Me."[135] The Apostle James says, "Count it all joy when you fall into divers trials, for the trial of your faith giveth it endurance";[136] that is, work the divine principle into the very substance of the mind. This surely is the great purpose of providence in the appointment of events with regard to individuals. Not a sparrow falls to the ground without God, and not an event happens without a particular reference to the state and character of the person to whom it happens. We have thus every day of our lives many direct and special messages from God to our souls. They are messages from God, and surely, we show Him small respect if we treat His messages as trifling things. They are full of importance. They are opportunities given to us of dying unto self and living unto God and holding communion with Him. In every one of them God says to us, "seek ye My face" and we ought to be ever ready with our answer, "Thy face,

135. John 15:4.
136. Jas 1:2–3.

Lord, will we seek."[137] With what an [awakening][138] of attention should we live if we *really* believed that every event is a voice from God and an opportunity of dying unto self that cannot be neglected without great guilt and great loss to our souls. My dear reader, allow me to repeat this to you. Every event that happens to us strengthens either the love of God or the principle of self within us because on every event we exercise our judgment or our feelings, and this we must do either according to the will of God or according to our own will.

Thus, we can never stand still for a moment—there is no rest from the conflict—we are continually taking part either with God or against God. There are but two ways in which man can walk towards eternity—the narrow way that leads to life and the broad way that leads to destruction. The first is the way of self-forgetting and God-pleasing—the second is the way of self-pleasing and God-forgetting. In one or other of these ways every man is walking. He is either resisting self or not. He may be doing nothing decidedly wrong according to the world's estimate of duty, but unless he is systematically denying himself and taking up his cross daily, he *cannot be* Christ's disciple for there is no room for Christ's love in a heart that refuses to give up self. Oh! if we felt as we ought that that only is good that draws us near to God, and that self is indeed the great bar that divides us from God and keeps us at a distance from Him, how easily should we be reconciled to those events that cross and thwart the principle of self-seeing that they weaken the bar which separates us from God, our only real good—we should then know that there is no evil but sin, and that everything else must be a blessing if it is received in the spirit of prayer. We are apt to lay our own faults upon events and to think that if our circumstances had been more favorable as we call it, we should have been more religious or more peaceful or more spiritually minded. The Apostle James meets all such complaints in this way.

> Let no man say when he is tempted, I am tempted of God, for God cannot be tempted with evil, neither tempteth He any man, but every man is tempted when he is drawn away of his own lust and enticed. Then when lust hath conceived it bringeth forth sin, and sin when it is finished, bringeth forth death. Do not err, my beloved brethren, in this matter—every appointment is gracious in its intention, and divinely fitted for its purpose, and

137. Ps 27:8.

138. Replaced "awakenedness."

cometh down from the Father of lights, with whom there is no variableness, neither shadow of turning.[139]

Practical religion consists in seeing God the Father of our Lord Jesus Christ in everything and in expecting a blessing from Him in everything and in being more concerned as to the spiritual improvement that we may draw from every event that befalls us than as to the nature of the event itself being either agreeable or disagreeable to us or, in other words, it consists in the spirit of dependence and of prayer.

Affliction is a great realizer in religion, or rather a great detector of the want of reality in religion. We, perhaps, thought ourselves Christians, and that we were founded on the rock, and now an affliction comes, and we shake like aspen leaves. Could this be if we were really on the rock? We thought fondly that God was the chosen portion of our souls, and that though all created things were taken from us, we had enough when we had Him, and yet when He crosses some desire of our hearts or removes some of His own gifts—a friend, perhaps, or even a little of the world's trash, we seem as if we had lost our all and cry after it as that Danite did after his idols,[140] and thus we learn the fact that our comfort before did not, as we idly supposed, flow from the eternal fountain (for that still remains to us) but had been drawn from perishing cisterns, and therefore, now that they are broken, we die of thirst. This is an important discovery, and it was to make this discovery to us that God sent the affliction. Let us then receive it in deep humility—let us receive it as a call from God to leave the creature behind us and go directly into his own more immediate presence, into His inner chamber. Reader, will you allow me to speak a word to you on this matter? Beware of occupying your mind as to how the affliction happened or how it might have been prevented. Think not of the oversight or folly or malice that may appear to you to have been the immediate occasion of it. God did it, and you must send away all second causes from your thought and carry the affliction to His throne of grace and cast it and yourself before Him and ask Him to save your soul and to deliver you from resting on any created portion and pray Him to become Himself your real and true and everlasting portion. Take care that this affliction be not lost. *Abide* in his presence and be jealous of receiving comfort from any other source. You may lose your affliction if you do. And oh! remember that holiness is of more importance than comfort. Be

139. Jas 1:13–17.
140. Judg 18.

still more anxious for profit from your affliction than for support under it. You are an immortal creature and eternity is your great concern. Holiness *is eternal* happiness—comfort may be the affair of *an hour*. And God sends affliction that we may become partakers of his holiness.

Let me conclude by saying that all is to be looked for and received from God. "Open thy mouth wide and I will fill it."[141] It is the soul that receives *all* from God that alone can feel itself to be the property of God—His property to guide and to command—His property to bless and to keep—His highly prized property purchased at no less a cost than the death of Christ for this very end that He might sanctify it in time and glorify it in eternity. The soul that feels this has peace. It does not make haste for it knows how secure it is. It possesses the secret of the Lord, that secret that does for all circumstances and contingences—that does for life, for death, for duty, for suffering—that gives the spirit of a pilgrim and yet a willing servant—that gives the foretaste of the joy of heaven as it is the commencement of the character of heaven.

Reader, farewell—I believe that what I have written is according to the word of God, and as far as it is so, I may look up to Him for a blessing on it. It would be an unspeakable joy to me to have any reason to think that it has been really honored by Him to be the bearer of a message to your soul. At all events, I trust it may not do you the injury of exciting the spirit of controversy in you. If you don't agree with it, lay it down and go to the Bible, and if you do agree with it, in like manner lay it down and go to the Bible and go in the spirit of prayer to Him whose word the Bible is and ask of Him, and He will lead you into all truth—He will give you living water.

THE END.

---

141. Ps 81:10.

PART TWO

Additional Readings from Thomas Erskine

Additional Readings from Thomas Erskine

Christin, the Gift of God's Love

Christ, the gift of God's present forgiving love to every man and woman, is the door through which alone we can enter into our provision of hope. Until we know the love of our Father's heart to us as manifested in Christ, the future must always be to us at best a dark and doubtful wilderness.

But when we know that all that we have conceived of our Father's love is as nothing to the reality—that He is indeed love itself—a love passing knowledge—a shoreless, boundless, bottomless ocean-fountain of love, of holy, sin hating, sin destroying love, which longs over us that we should be filled with itself—and be by it delivered from the power of evil—then, indeed, we are saved by hope for we know that love must triumph and fulfill all its counsel.[1]

Christlikeness, God's Ultimate Objective

[A] restoration to spiritual health or conformity to the Divine character is the *ultimate object* of God in His dealings with the children of men. Whatever else God has done with regard to men has been subsidiary and with a view to this. Even the unspeakable work of Christ and pardon freely offered through His cross have been but means to a further end, and that end is that the adopted children of the family of God might

---

1. Erskine, *Brazen Serpent*, 122–23.

be conformed to the likeness of their elder brother—that they might resemble Him in character and thus enter into His joy.[2]

Education, Not Probation

There are few religious phrases that have had such a power of darkening men's minds as to their true relation to God as the common phrase that we are here in a state of probation—under trial as it were. We are not in a state of trial. We are in a process of education directed by that eternal purpose of love which brought us into being. It is impossible to have a true confidence in God while we feel ourselves in a state of trial. We must necessarily regard Him not as a Father but as a Judge, and we must be occupied with the thought how we are to pass our trial. We know our own unworthiness, and though we know that we have a Savior, there must still be a degree of alarm in the thought of that judgment-seat. But when we have once realized the idea that we are in a process of education which God will carry on to its fulfilment however long it may take, we feel that the loving purpose of our Father is ever resting on us, and that the events of life are not appointed as testing us whether we will choose God's will or our own, but real lessons to train us into making the right choice. If probation is our thought, then forgiveness or receiving a favorable sentence is our object; if education is our thought, then progress in holiness is our object. If I believe myself in a state of education, every event, even death itself, becomes a manifestation of God's eternal purpose. On the probation system, Christ appears as the deliverer from a condemnation; on the education system, He appears as the deliverer from sin itself.[3]

The Meaning of Salvation

We should ask what is the meaning of the word *salvation*. For most assuredly the spirit and character of our religion will much depend on the signification which we attribute to it. If we really believe that the great object of the Savior's mission to this earth was to save men from their sins, we shall also believe that salvation means a deliverance not from punishment but from sin. And how is this to be affected? How can we escape from sin? I would answer that the only conceivable way is by ceasing

2. Hanna, *Letters*, 16.

3. Hanna, *Letters*, 128–29.

from sin, that is, by becoming righteous. And as we have seen that man's righteousness consists in filial trust, we seem to be conducted to the idea that Christ saves us from sin by revealing to us the trustworthiness of the Father.[4]

Erskine's "Barthian" View of Election

I believe that the presence of Jesus in us with His quickening (vivifying) Spirit gives to each of us the power, whether we use it or not, of joining and taking part with Him against the evils of our own hearts, and I believe that in as far as we do so, we become partakers of His nature and members of His body. I believe that Jesus is the one Elect, and that those who by thus taking part with Jesus become members of His body become also members of the election, and that those who continue to resist Him shut themselves out from the election.[5] In this way also I believe that, as Christ was really given to men immediately after the fall,[6] all are elect in Him, He being in them all, and all are reprobate or rejected in the first Adam, but that we can make either our election or our reprobation sure by joining ourselves either to the one party or the other. I believe that God takes the first step to every man, and draws every man by His Spirit, and that man's part is acceptance and yielding.[7]

Erskine on the Scriptures

There is a divine beauty and wisdom in the form in which God has chosen to communicate the knowledge of His character, which when duly considered, can scarcely fail of exciting gratitude and admiration. . . . [The Bible] presents a history of wondrous love in order to excite gratitude, of high and holy worth to attract veneration and esteem. It presents a view of danger to produce alarm, of refuge to confer peace and joy, and of eternal glory to animate hope.[8]

4. Erskine, *Spiritual Order*, 243.

5. This statement would be considered classic Barth if not for the fact that Erskine was writing a hundred years before Karl Barth.

6. Based on Erskine's reading of John 1:10.

7. Hanna, *Letters*, 228.

8. Erskine, *Remarks*, 40.

Not in Man's Own Strength

Let me not be misunderstood as if I said either that man can in his own strength turn to God or of his own origination would ever desire to do so—but man, since the gift of Christ, need not do anything in his own strength. The strength of God is communicated to him in the seed of the word sown in his heart, so that he may take hold of it, and walk with God, and it is only by his own willful refusal to use that strength that he is without it. Conversion is, indeed, man's first step in the spiritual life, but he never could have taken this step, nor could he ever rightly have been commanded to take it, unless God had first taken a step towards him. The Word, who was with God, and was God, and in whom there is life, has come into man's nature—into the whole mass of the nature—as a fountain of life to quicken every man, and as a living cord to draw man up to God. And shall we now speak and reason about man as if he were yet in the condition into which Adam's fall brought him before the Word was given, though now in him, "God is the Saviour of all men, specially of those who believe,"[9] and in Him also "the grace of God which bringeth salvation to all men hath appeared,"[10] and "where sin abounded, there hath grace much more abounded"?[11] Most assuredly there is in Jesus Christ a *general* salvation for the whole race inasmuch as in Him they are lifted again into that state of probation from which in Adam they had fallen, and are provided with spiritual strength to go through their probation, whether they use that strength or not. But none *personally* becomes a partaker of salvation, except by personally turning to God. And in like manner, there is in Jesus Christ a general election for the whole race—inasmuch as, in Him, they are lifted out of that state of reprobation into which in Adam they had fallen; but no one becomes personally elect except by his personally receiving Christ into his heart.[12]

9. 1 Tim 4:10.

10. Erskine is here providing his own literal translation of Titus 2:11. Both the NRSV and the NASB agree with Erskine's rendering of the verse.

11. Rom 5:20.

12. Erskine, *Election*, 141–43.

The Role of Conscience

I hope that my reader will see that in thus requiring that what we learn from the Bible should harmonize with the light in our consciences, I am not detracting from the true authority of the inspired Book, but only putting it in its true place. What that place is, is distinctly marked in 2 Timothy 3:16, "All Scripture which is given by inspiration of God, is also profitable, for doctrine, for reproof, for correction, for instruction in righteousness, that the man of God may be perfect, thoroughly furnished unto all good works." Now it is manifest that unless in my own conscience I am perceiving the righteousness of the will of God revealed in any doctrine, I cannot be instructed in righteousness by it. For instruction in righteousness must mean here the instruction received in the conscience, that is, the awakening and nourishing within me of the perception and love of righteousness, which cannot take place when I am receiving a doctrine in the way of submission to authority, without really perceiving the righteousness that is in it.[13]

The Three Wills Within

Thus, every man has in his present state of trial three distinct wills within him of which he is himself conscious—first, the will of God striving with his conscience; second, the will of Satan or self, ruling in his members; and third, the elective will, in his own personality, which determines with which of the other two wills he shall side. This last will, though it has this peculiar prerogative, is yet never itself the dominant will, it only chooses which of the other two shall be dominant.[14]

God's Grace Is Available to All

When we see the two natures of flesh and spirit, *so* in every man that he may join himself to either of them and thus become either reprobate or elect, we see the root of the doctrine of election. And when we see rightly the gift of Christ, we shall see that as He is the true *light* which lights every man, so also there is in Him a communication of *life* to every man.

13. Erskine, *Election*, xi.
14. Erskine, *Election*, 281.

For "in Him was *life*; and *the life* was *the light of men*";[15] and thus, the light that lights every man is *a living* light—a light whereby he may live. And thus, by the entrance of the word into our flesh, not only has God been brought near to us as an *object* of trust and love, but also His *living* Spirit, the divine nature, has been communicated to us *subjectively* as a capacity of embracing God whether we exercise it or not.[16]

Erskine's Christology

Jesus took the flesh, just as the "children" have it (Heb 2:14), but that does not make Him a sinner for as He was without sin in a sinful world, so He was without sin in a sinful nature. And how was He so? Was it not by a continual accordance of His whole life with that word, "not My will, but Thine be done"? Was it not by a continual refusal to live to the flesh and a continual choosing to live to the Spirit? And how did He condemn sin in the flesh[17] but by thus living and by submitting Himself to the sentence of sorrow and death laid on the flesh, not merely as a righteous judgment, but as a gracious provision by which the Fatherly love of God would lead those who in filial confidence submit to it out from the horrible pit into which the nature had fallen? And the Father sealed the condemnation of the sin in the flesh by raising from the dead, without the touch of corruption, Him who had thus lived *in* the flesh without ever consenting to live *to* it.

It was thus that Jesus condemned sin in the flesh, and it was through His condemnation of it that the Father condemned it—for the Father could only condemn it as He desired to do, namely in a way consistent with the salvation of men, by doing it through the cooperation of man's own will, and therefore He had sent His own Son into the flesh, not only to prove His love to man, but also that He might have a man, a partaker of the flesh, who would go along with Him in his condemnation of the sin in it, and who would be a witness to His brethren from His own experience that God's will is man's only *life* as it is his only *guide*, and that sorrow and death when received in Filial confidence, are the medicine of the soul, and the way out of the corruption, and who would not only be a witness to them of these things, but would also be in them and to them a fountain

15. John 1:4.

16. Erskine, *Election*, 61.

17. Erskine's thoughts are flowing from Rom 8:3–4.

of the same filial life by the strength of which He himself had done this work enabling all of them who would receive it to yield themselves unto God and to become co-operators with Him and co-witnesses with Him of the same truth.[18]

Erskine's Personal Views on the Salvation of All

Undated letter to J. Craig, author of the pamphlet "The Final Salvation of All Men from Sin"

Dear Sir,

Your epistle on the "Final Salvation of All Men from Sin" has been put into my hands by a friend who knew that the principles contained in it are those with which I have long concurred and sympathized, and having read it, I cannot help reaching out to you a brotherly hand and saying, God speed you!

The title of your pamphlet has been, I think, well chosen. It is not a deliverance from punishment, but a deliverance from sin that you desire or expect. All punishment appointed by God, whether it be the natural result of sin or any superadded chastisement, is intended by Him "for our profit, that we may be partakers of His holiness,"[19] so that a deliverance from punishment, instead of being a thing to be desired, would, in fact, be equivalent to the deliverance of a sick man from the necessary and wise prescription of a skillful physician. This is the revealed purpose of punishment—a purpose agreeing with the character of God and with the relation in which He stands to men. He is the "righteous Father"[20]—"the Father of the spirits of all flesh,"[21] "who willeth not the death of a sinner, but that all should come to repentance."[22] Let uphold fast the purpose of God in all punishment,[23] and remember that as it is the purpose of Him

18. Erskine, *Election*, 368–69.

19. Heb 12:10.

20. John 17:25.

21. Num 16:22; 27:16.

22. 2 Pet 3:9.

23. Even as a young Calvinist, Erskine did not see retributive justice as a necessary attribute of God. Shortly before he died, he wrote in a letter to John Young that the first text to set him on the road to this conclusion was Ps 25:8. *The Message* captures what Erskine saw in this verse. *Because* "God is fair and just; He corrects the misdirected, Sends them in the right direction." In Ps 107, Erskine saw corroborating evidence that

who changes not, but who is the same yesterday, today, and forever, it cannot be a purpose confined to any one stage of our being, but must extend over all the stages, and the whole duration of our being. It is surely most unreasonable to suppose that God should change His manner of dealing with us as soon as we quit this world, and that if we have resisted up to that moment His gracious endeavors to teach us righteousness, He should at once abandon the purpose for which He created us and redeemed us and give us over to the everlasting bondage of sin. Do we not feel that such a supposition is too horrible—that it is most dishonoring to Him who has said, "I will never leave thee, nor forsake thee,"[24] and, "The mountains shall depart, and the hills be removed, but My kindness shall not depart from thee, neither shall the covenant of My peace be removed, saith the LORD that hath mercy on thee"?[25]

This reasoning agrees with the argument presented to us in the 5th chapter of the Epistle to the Romans where the Apostle, in setting forth the fullness of the redemption by Christ, declares that the benefit through Him is in extent, parallel to the evil introduced by Adam, that is, that as the evil affects all without exception, so the blessing embraces all without exception. Let anyone read the 12th and 18th verses of that chapter as if in juxtaposition,[26] which they really are by construction, and he will find himself constrained to admit that this and nothing less could have been the meaning of the writer. Indeed, through the whole chapter there is a preponderating advantage thrown into the scale of the redemption to the effect that not only were the evils of the fall met by the salvation of Christ, but that the gain far surpassed the loss, so that it is really contrary to sound criticism to hold that in that most [word unclear] and most remarkable passage where the comparative results of the fall and the restoration are expressly considered, any ground is allowed or given for a doubt as to the final salvation of the whole human race. The 11th chapter of that Epistle is pervaded by the same doctrine being a declaration that God's election does not affect the truth and certainty of the final salvation

---

God only punishes out of love with the goal of restoring sinners to a right relationship with Himself.

24. Heb 13:5.

25. Isa 54:10.

26. Rom 5:12—"Therefore, just as sin came into the world through one man, and death came through sin, and so death spread to all because all have sinned. . . ." Verse 18 "Therefore just as one man's trespass led to condemnation for all, so one man's act of righteousness leads to justification and life for all" (NRSV).

of men but relates to the temporary use that He makes of individuals or nations to accomplish the ends of His government. I know well that most people in this country feel that all such arguments and expositions are met and overturned by the solemn words of our Lord in the 25th chapter Matthew, and by other passages of a like import. I feel, on the contrary, that the passages which I have quoted from the Epistle to the Romans ought really to be considered as the ruling passages on the question, and that those from St. Matthew and others of the same class should be explained by them and in accordance with them because in them the fall and the restoration are expressly compared with each other in their whole results, and the entire superiority claimed for the restoration in amount of benefit and entire equality in point of extent, all which would seem to me to be utterly nullified by the fact of a single human spirit being abandoned and consigned to a permanent state of sin and misery. I therefore understand that awful scene represented in St. Matthew as declaring the certainty of the connection between sin and misery, but not as a finality. I do not believe that *aiōniŏs*, the Greek word rendered "eternal" and "everlasting" by our translators, really has that meaning.[27] I believe that it refers to man's essential or spiritual state and not to time, either finite or infinite. Eternal life is living in the love of God; eternal death is living in self, so that a man may be in eternal life or in eternal death for ten minutes as he changes from the one state to the other.

There is no lack of arguments for the general view that I have taken of this subject drawn either from conscience or the Scriptures or both. There is one which cannot but have great weight with all who fairly consider it. Throughout even the Old Testament, God is more constantly presented to us as a Father than in any other character, and in the New, our Lord speaks of it as the chief purpose of His appearance in this world to reveal His Father as the Father of the whole human race. In both, frequent appeals are made to our sense of the love and desires and obligations of an earthly parent towards his children in order to impress on us the nature of the relation in which God stands to each one of us, and very frequently these appeals are accompanied with the assurance that the love of the human parent is but a faint reflection of the love of the Heavenly Father. What can be more touching than the appeal in the prophet Isaiah? "Can a woman forget her sucking child, that she should not have compassion on the son of her womb? yea, they may forget, yet will not

27. See Vincent, *Word Studies*, vol. IV, 58–62 or Barclay, *More New Testament Words*, 24–32 for more detailed discussion of this subject.

I forget thee."[28] The parallel passage in the New Testament is this: "If ye then, being evil, know how to give good gifts to your children, how much more will your Heavenly Father give!"[29] But we all feel that the first and ever-during duty of a father is to endeavor to make his child righteous. A righteous father must always do this. The moment he ceases to do this, he ceases to be a righteous father. However the son transgresses, we never feel that the father's obligation to try to bring him back can be dissolved. And the righteous father's heart goes along with his obligation. He could not give up his son although the whole world agreed that he had done all that could be done for him, and that it was useless to try any more. And shall we not reason confidently that the righteous Heavenly Father will do exceedingly abundantly above all that the righteous earthly father can either desire or effect? But does this desire for the righteousness of his child in the heart of the earthly father terminate with the child's life? Although he is only the father of his body, does he not yearn after the soul of his son, who has been, perhaps, cut off suddenly in the midst of sin and thoughtlessness? He does indeed yearn after his soul and carries it on his heart a heavy burden mourning all his life long and wavering between hope and fear as to what his everlasting lot may be. The righteous earthly father being only the father of the child's body feels thus and acts thus, and can we suppose that the Father of the spirits of all flesh will throw off His care for the souls of His children when they leave this world because they have during their stay here resisted His efforts to make them righteous? The supposition seems monstrous and incredible and in truth could not be acquiesced in by any human being were it not for certain false ideas concerning the justice or righteousness of God.

I believe that love and righteousness and justice in God mean exactly the same thing, namely a desire to bring His whole moral creation into a participation of His own character and His own blessedness. He has made us capable of this, and He will not cease from using the best means for accomplishing it in us all. When I think of God making a creature of such capacities, it seems to me almost blasphemous to suppose that He will throw it from Him into everlasting darkness because it has resisted His gracious purposes towards it for the natural period of human life. No, He who waited so long for the formation of a piece of old red sandstone will surely wait with much long-suffering for the perfecting of a human spirit.

28. Isa 49:15.

29. Matt 7:11.

I have found myself helped in taking hold of this hope by understanding that God really made man that He might educate Him, not that He might try him. If we suppose man to be merely on his trial here, we more readily adopt the idea of a final judgment coming after the day of trial is over. But if we suppose man to be created, not to be tried, but to be educated, we cannot believe that the education is to terminate with this life considering that there is so large a proportion of the human race who die in infancy, and that of those who survive that period there are so many who can scarcely be said to receive any education at all, and that so few—not one in a million—appear to benefit by their education. That, as there are great judgment days in this world, so there will be great judgment days in the other world, I have no doubt, but I believe that they are all subservient to the grand purpose of spiritual education. We are judged in order to be thereby educated. We are not educated that we may be judged. I believe that each individual human being has been created to fill a particular place in the great body of Jesus Christ, and that a special education is needed to fit each one for his place. Whilst we are ignorant of the destined place of each, it must of course be impossible for us to understand the wonderful variety of treatment through which the great Teacher is conducting all by a right way to the right end. But He knows and does what is best and wisest, and may there not be a necessity in some cases for treatment which can only be had on the other side of the grave? And shall we in our short-sightedness consider Him debarred from any such treatment?

I cannot believe that any human being can be beyond the reach of God's grace and the sanctifying power of His Spirit. And if all are within His reach, is it possible to suppose that He will allow any to remain unsanctified? Is not the love revealed in Jesus Christ a love unlimited, unbounded, which will not leave undone anything that love could desire? It was surely nothing other than the complete and universal triumph of that love that Paul was contemplating when he cried out, "Oh the depth of the riches both of the wisdom and knowledge of God!" (Rom 11:33).

Let me conclude now by saying that I am persuaded that this doctrine that you advocate is the only sufficient ground for an entire confidence in God, which shall at the same time be a righteous confidence. According to it, God created man that he might be a partaker in His own holiness as the only right and blessed state possible for him. If I truly apprehend this—if I truly apprehend that righteousness and blessedness are one and the same thing, and just the very thing I most need—I shall rejoice to know that God desires my righteousness, and if I further know that He will never cease to desire it and to insist upon it, and that all His dealings with me are for this one end, then I can have an entire confidence in Him as desiring for me the very thing I desire for myself. I shall feel that I am perfectly safe in His hand, that I could not be so safe in any other hand for that, as He desires the best thing for me, so He alone knows and can use the best means of accomplishing it in me. Thus, I can actually adopt the sentiment of the Psalmist and say, "Thou art my strong habitation, whereunto I may continually resort. Thou hast given commandment to save me, for Thou art my rock and fortress."[30] And I can adopt these words without any feeling of self-trust because my confidence has no back look to myself but rests simply on God. The greatest sinner upon earth might at once adopt those words if he only saw that righteousness was his true and only possible blessedness and that God would never cease desiring this righteousness for him. I am fully persuaded that the real meaning of believing in Jesus Christ is believing in this eternal purpose of God, the purpose of making us living members of the body of His Son. And as this blessed faith helps me to love God and trust Him for myself, so it helps me to love my fellow creatures because it assures me that however debased and unlovable they may be at present, yet the time is coming when they shall all be living members of Christ's body, partakers in the holiness and beauty and blessedness of their Lord.

—I remain, dear sir, Yours truly, T. Erskine[31]

30. Ps 71:1.

31. Hanna, *Letters*, 422–29.

Bibliography

Campbell, John McLeod. *Reminiscences and Reflections: Referring to His Early Ministry in the Parish of Row, 1825–31.* London: Macmillan, 1873.

Barclay, William. *More New Testament Words.* London: SCM, 1958.

Erskine, Thomas. *The Brazen Serpent: Or, Life Coming through Death.* Edinburgh: Waugh & Innes, 1831.

———. *The Doctrine of Election and Its Connection with the General Tenor of Christianity, Illustrated from Many Parts of Scripture and Especially from the Epistle to the Romans.* London: James Duncan, 1837.

———. "The Purpose of God in the Creation of Man." Edinburgh: Edmonston and Douglas, 1870.

———. *Remarks on the Internal Evidence for the Truth of Revealed Religion.* Edinburgh: Waugh & Innes, 1820.

———. "Salvation." In *The Letters of the Rev. Samuel Rutherford, Late Professor of Divinity at St. Andrews. With an Introductory Essay by Thomas Erskine, Esq.* Glasgow: Chalmers and Collins, 1825.

———. *The Spiritual Order and Other Papers: Selected from the Manuscripts of the Late Thomas Erskine of Linlathen.* 3rd ed. Edinburgh: David Douglas, 1884.

———. *The Unconditional Freeness of the Gospel: In Three Essays.* Edinburgh: Waugh and Innes, 1828.

Drummond, A. L., and J. Bulloch. *The Scottish Church 1688–1843.* Edinburgh: St Andrew's Press, 1973.

Franks, R. S. *A History of the Doctrine of the Work of Christ in Its Ecclesiastical Development.* London: Hodder and Stoughton, n.d. (c. 1930).

Hanna, William. *Letters of Thomas Erskine of Linlathen.* 2nd ed. Edinburgh: David Douglas, 1878.

Hart, Trevor A. *Teaching Father: Introduction to the Theology of Thomas Erskine of Linlathen.* Edinburgh: Saint Andrew's Press, 1993.

Henderson, Henry F. *Erskine of Linlathen: Selections and Biography.* Edinburgh: Oliphant Anderson & Ferrier, 1899.

Horrocks, Don. *Laws of the Spiritual Order: Innovation and Reconstruction in the Soteriology of Thomas Erskine of Linlathen.* Studies in Evangelical History and Thought. Carlisle, UK: Paternoster, 2004. Reprint, Eugene, OR: Wipf & Stock, 2007.

Keyser, David J. "A Critical Analysis of the Pneumatology of Thomas Erskine of Linlathen." PhD diss., University of St Andrews, 2004.

Needham, Nicholas R. *Thomas Erskine of Linlathen: His Life and Theology 1788–1837.* Edinburgh: Rutherford House, 1990.

Jinkins, Michael. "Campbell, John McLeod (1800–72)." In *The Dictionary of Historical Theology*, edited by Trevor A. Hart et al., 106–8. Grand Rapids: Eerdmans, 2000.

Reardon, Bernard M. G. *Religious Thought in the Victoria Age: A Survey from Coleridge to Gore.* 2nd ed. London: Longman, 1995.

Reid, Robert A. "The Influence, Direct and Indirect, of the Writings of Erskine of Linlathen on Religious Thought in Scotland." PhD diss., University of Edinburgh, 1930.

Storr, V. F. *The Development of English Theology in the Nineteenth Century.* London: Longmans, Green & Co., 1913.

Story, Robert Herbert. *The Apostolic Ministry in the Scottish Church.* Edinburgh: William Blackwood and Sons, 1897.

Tulloch, J. *Movements of Religious Thought in Britain during the Nineteenth Century.* London: Longmans, Green & Co., 1885.

Torrance, Thomas F. *Theology in Reconciliation: Essays towards Evangelical and Catholic Unity in East and West.* London: Chapman, 1975.

Winslow, Donald R. *Thomas Erskine: Advocate for the Character of God.* Lanham, MD: University Press of America, 1993.

Vincent, Marvin R. *Vincent's Word Studies in the New Testament, Volume IV.* Peabody, MA: Hendrickson, 1923.

Young, Sue. "Thomas Erskine 1788–1870." https://www.sueyounghistories.com/2009-05-09-thomas-erskine-1788-1870/.

www.ingramcontent.com/pod-product-compliance
Lightning Source LLC
Chambersburg PA
CBHW070743030726
47601CB00001B/123